OPERATION OVERLORD

Cornwall & Preparation for the D-Day Landings

RODERICK DE NORMANN

Published by Truran

Truran is an imprint of Tor Mark,
United Downs Industrial Estate,
St Day, Redruth, Cornwall TR16 5HY

www.tormark.co.uk

Published 2019

ISBN 978 1 85022 258 3

Text: © Roderick de Normann

Printed and bound in Great Britain
by Cambrian Printers

Front Cover:
– 6th Special Engineer Brigade on board LST-325 with
St Mawes Castle in the background
– US Convoy on a widened Cornish Road

Title Page:
– 'SeaBees', Lieutenant Commander Shepler painting

This Page:
– Exercise Duck 1. March down through Falmouth

Reverse Back Cover:
– US Landing Craft Vehicle/Personnel come
ashore at Slapton Sands

CONTENTS

IN GOD'S GOOD TIME...

O n the 4th of June, 1940, the newly installed British Prime Minister Winston Churchill stood up in the House of Commons to address a packed chamber. Churchill went on to make his famous 'We will fight them on the beaches...' promise. Not often quoted, however, are the last few lines from that speech; he said '...our Empire beyond the seas, guarded by the British Fleet, would carry on the struggle until in God's good time the New World, with all its power and might, steps forth to the rescue and liberation of the Old'.

Prophetic words; in Cornwall 'God's good time' was to last four years to the day. On the 5th June 1944, thirty-eight Landing Ships (Tank) – or LSTs – departed from the Fal Estuary in South Cornwall. Others joined them from the Helford River, the port at Fowey and the River Tamar. Escorted by the Royal Navy and numerous smaller craft, these LSTs were loaded with soldiers from the New World – mostly Americans of the 1st and 29th Infantry Divisions. They took with them the initial elements of two artificial Mulberry harbours and a number of floating pontoons, known as 'Rhino Ferries'.

*

IN THE BEGINNING...

When Prime Minister Neville Chamberlain announced to the world that Great Britain had declared war against Germany on the 3rd September 1939, the Army was woefully ill prepared. Although many did not believe that a future war would be similar to that of 1914-1918, the lessons that should have been learnt were either ignored or forgotten. The Army in particular had suffered twenty years of under-funding and substantial cuts.

One of the first operations undertaken was to move the British Expeditionary Force (BEF) across the Channel and into France. In scenes that would be almost identical to those in 1944, many Southern ports facilitated the deployment. Falmouth saw elements of the 3rd Infantry Division move into a rest camp administered by elements of the 96th (Royal Devon Yeomanry) Field Regiment, Royal Artillery between the 23rd September to the 1st October, 1939. Barely eight months later, many would be back.

The fall of France in 1940 gave way to a very real threat of invasion of the UK, but German eyes were on bigger prizes. In 1941 the initial successes of the German invasion of Soviet Russia and Rommel in North Africa threatened India. To make matters worse, the Japanese launched their attacks in the Far East during December 1941, including the infamous attack on the US Pacific Fleet at Pearl Harbour. Hong Kong, Singapore and the Philippines soon fell and by mid-1942, even the North Coast of Australia was under threat of invasion.

The Japanese attacks, however, proved to be the silver linings within some very dark clouds. Pearl Harbour demanded that American President Franklin D. Roosevelt immediately declare war on Japan and in response, Germany and Italy declared war on the United States. With American entry into the war, strategic victory would be – in Churchill's words – based on a '…well-grounded confidence in the final outcome'.

PRESIDENT ROOSEVELT SIGNS THE AMERICAN DECLARATION OF WAR AGAINST GERMANY AND ITALY ON 11TH DECEMBER 1941. (US LIBRARY OF CONGRESS)

Two weeks later on the 20th December 1941, Roosevelt and Churchill met in Washington where three highly important decisions were made:

- *That a UK / US Joint Chiefs of Staff Committee would be established to conduct the strategic military operations, including liaison with Stalin in Russia,*

- *The strategic policy would primarily concentrate on 'Germany first' as the greater danger,*

- *The strategic aim would be for the unconditional surrender of all Axis Forces through invasion of first Germany and then Japan.*

Perhaps a trifle naively at the time, the US believed that a cross-channel attack into occupied France could and should be undertaken as soon as possible. This was also being urged by Stalin. Two plans were considered. The first was Operation SLEDGEHAMMER, which envisaged a cross-channel attack onto the Cherbourg Peninsular in late autumn 1942 with a break-out in the Spring of 1943. The second was Operation ROUNDUP, planned for summer 1943 and using three divisions into Normandy.

The British had grave doubts about both plans and their fears were dramatically reinforced after the repulse of the Canadian raid against the French port of Dieppe in August 1942. The heavy casualties suffered taught the Allies three major lessons:

- *Any future invasion could not hope to capture a major sea port intact.*

- *Infantry disembarking onto a beach could not hope to survive without both armoured and engineer support.*

- *Such an attack could not hope for success without the flanks being secured.*

*

Although America did not declare itself at war with Germany until the 8th December 1941, there had been American troops in the United Kingdom for over a year. On the 15th August 1940, US Rear Admiral Robert L. Ghormley and a small staff arrived in London. Admiral Ghormley had been appointed as a Special Observer by the US War Department, working out of the American Embassy in Grosvenor Square. This was a delicate task as the United States was still overtly neutral with many American politicians demanding that the country stays so.

On initially visiting the Admiralty in London, Ghormley was briefed on the so-called 'Bailey Committee', under the chairmanship of Admiral Sir Sidney Bailey RN.

This had been established for three principal reasons:

- *To define areas of specific British and US naval operations.*

- *To define and discuss naval assistance required from the US.*

- *To demarcate British and American responsibilities in such areas.*

Rear Admiral Ghormley's reporting was highly regarded back in Washington, so much so that the War Department went on to despatch Major General James E. Chaney, US Army Air Force, to London to act as a Special Army Observer.

US REAR ADMIRAL ROBERT L. GHORMLEY, PHOTOGRAPHED IN 1942 AS A VICE ADMIRAL, THE SPECIAL OBSERVER IN THE UK FOR THE US WAR DEPARTMENT DURING THE BATTLE OF BRITAIN, SUMMER 1940. (US NAVAL HISTORY & HERITAGE COMMAND)

General Chaney was offered unfettered access throughout the British Army and Royal Air Force. This allowed him to prepare a significant report that went back to Washington, arriving on the 15th December 1940. In this, Chaney stated that the RAF was winning the Battle of Britain and that the British Government '…was determined to, and capable of, waging the war as a whole to a victorious conclusion'.

Such praise for the British stance brought swift reward. US President Roosevelt sent his close friend and confident Harry Hopkins to London. He was to act as the President's personal representative and '...catalytic agent...'. Although he had no negotiating authority, he was tasked to '...talk with everyone who mattered...'. British Prime Minister Winston Churchill ensured he saw everything and this he did, extending his mission from one week to three.

HARRY HOPKINS, US PRESIDENT ROOSEVELT'S 'CATALYTIC AGENT', FOLLOWING HIS VISIT TO ENGLAND IN JANUARY 1941. (US LIBRARY OF CONGRESS)

On the 29th January 1941, as Mr Hopkins wrapped up his tour in the UK, military representatives from America, Britain and Canada met secretly in Washington to discuss plans for the future possibility that America would enter the war. Known as 'ABC', these talks continued for two months, resulting in a number of strategic decisions that were to remain relevant for the remainder of the war.

The first of these was the principle of 'Germany first'. Atlantic convoys would need protection and US naval forces would need to use bases in the UK. In addition, both the UK and US agreed that the latter would build a base in Greenland for convoy protection with the UK operating out of Iceland, which had been first occupied by the Canadians and then the British after Germany had overrun Norway in April 1940.

Second, it was agreed that, in the event of America entering the war, Northern Ireland would be garrisoned by US troops in order to allow the deployment of better-trained British troops abroad. For such a plan, the Americans would require a base or bases through which they could land. Coinciding with the US Congress passing the 'Lend-Lease' Act in March 1941, American military surveyors chose Londonderry in Northern Ireland and Rosneath in Scotland as the first two bases for construction. Despite being built in Britain, these bases were essentially '…built by American contractors with American money for American use'.

*

Following the attack on Pearl Harbour on the 7th December 1941, Britain declared war on Japan on the 8th December, a few hours before the Americans themselves. Both were quickly followed by Canada and the Netherlands. Taken totally by surprise, Hitler issued an immediate order that the U-Boat fleet was to attack any American vessels they came across. This was three days before Germany and Italy officially declared war themselves on the United States. President Roosevelt, of course, reciprocated.

Alongside the declaration of war, the US Congress '…voted for the despatch of American forces to any part of the world'. And this they did. On the 17th January 1942, the American minelayer, USS Albatross, docked in the new US naval base at Londonderry. She was soon followed by the first American troops of the new Northern Ireland garrison, who landed in Belfast on the 26th January 1942. The floodgates were now opening.

*

In all his dealings with Washington, Churchill noted that although the Americans – lead by the Chief of Staff, General George C. Marshall – were very keen to confront the enemy across both the Atlantic and Pacific oceans, shipping constraints would deny them the ability to do so in 1942. Manpower was also a problem as the American Army only mustered 35 divisions in total, many with only basic training.

The British Prime Minister emphasised the American view that Great Britain was '…an essential fortress of the United Nations. It is indeed the only place where the war can be lost in the critical campaign of 1942…'. As such, the deployment of several American divisions to Northern Ireland and replacing a British division in Iceland with an American one was more than welcome.

Looking forward to 1943, Churchill noted that Congress had agreed to huge increases in the production of vehicles, aircraft and munitions. More importantly, recent and future American ship-building programmes would allow for greater troop movement, perhaps resulting in large offensive operations by the summer of that year. To that end, Churchill declared '(this) should be carefully studied'.

And studied it was. American and British planning staffs began their work on Operations SLEDGEHAMMER and ROUNDUP in what Churchill reportedly described as '…marching ahead together in a noble brotherhood of arms…'. Meanwhile the Americans looked at the huge logistical problem of moving enough men and materiel into – or onto – the British Isles in an operation the Americans called BOLERO.

*

In January 1943, Churchill and Roosevelt again met in Casablanca, Morocco. Despite the continued clamour for a 'Second Front', they agreed that conditions were not yet ready for a cross-channel attack, although they did make two further decisions; first to reinforce the current success in North Africa by invading Sicily using a full Allied invasion force of British, Canadian and American troops and second, that they would form a joint British and American staff to begin the detailed planning necessary for the Second Front, that now would be postponed until 1944.

PRIME MINISTER CHURCHILL AND PRESIDENT ROOSEVELT SURROUNDED BY THEIR SENIOR MILITARY STAFFS IN CASABLANCA, JANUARY 1943. (US LIBRARY OF CONGRESS)

JOSEF STALIN, FRANKLIN D. ROOSEVELT & WINSTON CHURCHILL IN TEHRAN, JANUARY 1943. (US LIBRARY OF CONGRESS)

The planners first came together in March 1943, under the command of the Chief of Staff's Committee to the Supreme Allied Commander and the planning team soon became known as COSSAC. For security and to reflect the new joint UK/US planning, the name of the operation was changed from ROUNDUP to OVERLORD.

COSSAC's initial plans were drawn up by August 1943 and presented to Churchill and Roosevelt at a conference in Quebec, Canada. COSSAC set the date for invasion as the 1st May 1944.

November 1943 saw a further meeting of Allied leaders including, for the first time, Josef Stalin. This time, they met in Tehran, Persia (now Iran). The latter demanded to know when the Second Front would open and who was to be the Supreme Allied Commander; he was briefed on the plan but told the commander had yet to be decided.

In December 1943, supreme command went to US General Dwight D. Eisenhower. Under him would be three British commanders for land, sea and air operations. General Bernard Montgomery was to be the principle ground commander. Not only would he be in command of the landings in Normandy, he was also to be responsible for the build-up of forces prior to any break-out towards Germany. To get the troops onto the beaches in Northern France would demand a separate, perhaps even more complex, naval operation – codenamed NEPTUNE. This was to be commanded by Admiral Sir Bertram Ramsey. Finally, all air operations came under the command of Air Chief Marshall Trafford Leigh-Mallory. This team was to remain together until September 1944 when it was subsumed into a command structure that was predominately American following the landings in Southern France during August 1944.

GENERAL EISENHOWER PHOTOGRAPHED AT HIS DESK ON THE 31ST DECEMBER, 1943. THIS WAS THE DAY THAT IT WAS OFFICIALLY ANNOUNCED THAT HE WAS TO BE THE SUPREME COMMANDER, ALLIED EXPEDITIONARY FORCES. IN FACT THE DECISION HAD BEEN TAKEN BY PRESIDENT ROOSEVELT ON THE EVENING OF THE 6TH DECEMBER 1943, EXACTLY TWO YEARS AFTER THE PEARL HABOUR ATTACK. (US NAVAL HISTORY & HERITAGE COMMAND)

1

DECISIONS, DECISIONS, DECISIONS...

Operation BOLERO – or the 'Marshall Memorandum' as the British called it after its chief designer US General George C. Marshall, the Head of the US Joint Chiefs of Staff – would support an attack into Europe using a combined Allied force of some 48 Divisions, supported by 5,800 aircraft. The US was looking to provide 1,000,000 men of which the main proportion would make up thirty combat divisions. They would also provide 3,250 combat aircraft. If the British could provide the eighteen remaining divisions and 2,550 aircraft, then the combined force would be large enough to secure air superiority in order to invade on a six-division front between Le Havre and Boulogne. The Americans suggested this could be achieved by the 1st April 1943.

GENERAL GEORGE C. MARSHALL, ONE OF THE MOST FUNDAMENTALLY IMPORTANT DECISION MAKERS IN WORLD WAR 2. (THE HYPER TEXT HISTORIES)

On the 14th April 1942, the British Cabinet and Chiefs of Staff formally accepted the 'Marshall Memorandum'. They agreed that planning for an attack in 1943 should proceed immediately. As such, the BOLERO/ROUNDUP plan became official policy for the Allies.

American planning fell to the Operations Division (OPD) working directly to the US Chief of Staff, General Marshall. As fate would have it, the OPD Chief was none other than Brigadier-General Dwight D. Eisenhower. On 23rd June 1942, he was both promoted to Commanding General, US European Theatre of Operations and set off for London.

With London and Washington in firm agreement of the necessary strategic way forward, the onerous task of assembling, training and maintaining the invasion forces began. With so many men, vehicles and stores about to arrive in the UK, every spare foot of space would have to be used wisely.

The American military logistics organisation that would oversee BOLERO was the Service of Supply (SOS), later renamed the Army Service Forces (ASF). SOS came into existence on the 9th March 1942, after the passing of Presidential Order 9082 designed to reorganise the US Army and the War Department. This had been issued on the 28th February and the first SOS European Theatre of Operations (SOS-ETO) elements that would oversee the movement of US forces into Britain arrived on the 24th May 1942 under the command of Major General John CH Lee.

MAJOR GENERAL JOHN CH LEE WAS APPOINTED COMMANDER, SERVICES OF SUPPLY (SOS) IN MAY 1942. HE BECAME COMMANDER, THEATRE SERVICE FORCES, EUROPEAN THEATRE (TSFET) ON PROMOTION TO LIEUTENANT GENERAL IN FEBRUARY 1944. (US NATIONAL ARCHIVES & RECORDS ADMINISTRATION)

In essence, General Lee commanded the American logistics chain. SOS would be the static framework through which the combat troops would move. As such, SOS comprised what the Americans called their 'technical services'; engineers, signals, ordnance, quartermasters, chemical defence troops and the medical chain. In addition, a new Transport Corps was formed to oversee all ports of embarkation and disembarkation, all military road regulations and the military use of all railway facilities.

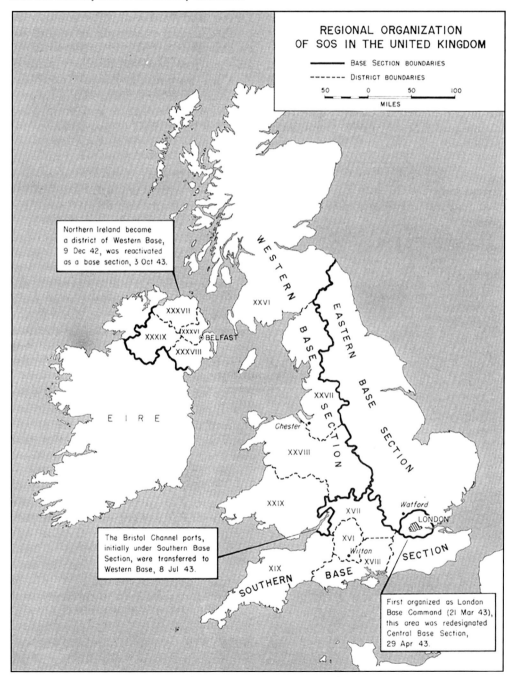

MAP – REGIONAL SOS COMMANDS. (THE HYPER TEXT HISTORIES)

In a similar vein to the British commands, SOS-ETO divided the UK into six Base Sections: Northern Ireland, Western including Wales and Scotland, Eastern, Central around London, South Eastern and Southern. Southern Base Section (SnBS) was to be where the bulk of US combat troops would be accommodated. SnBS roughly stretched from Southampton, West to Lands End. SnBS was itself divided into thirteen districts, with Somerset, Devon and Cornwall making up the Western District, later renamed XIX District.

It is interesting to note that, on crossing the Atlantic, the American soldiers only carried their personal items, clothing and weapon or side arm. Everything else they would require was to be provided once they reached their final destination. As such therefore, each district within SnBS was required to provide not only sufficient accommodation and storage space for the troops and their equipment once issued, but also sufficient space to store the heavier equipment prior to issue.

Many of the existing British camps, barracks or garrisons within SnBS were handed over to the Americans. Where military accommodation was not available, billeting was found in private homes. This was not difficult to find as the Americans paid just over $4.20 a day for the privilege, with many of those billeted able to supplement the meagre English food supplies caused by national rationing with excellent US Army rations.

By the 1st May 1944, there was living accommodation for 1,182,758 US ground troops in the United Kingdom, of which 537,500 were in the SnBS. The Americans alone had access to 119,100 hospital beds and some 19,905,070 square feet of covered storage and workshop space. 3,000 properties were completely taken over by the Americans in 1,108 separate towns and villages. In addition, there were 43,345,575 square feet of open storage and hard-standing for 173,325 tons of petrol, oil and lubricants (POL), 448,100 tons of ammunition of all calibres and vehicle parks for 48,350 vehicles, both tracked and wheeled. Add to these the figures for the US Navy and US Army Air Force, there is ample understanding of the 1944 sobriquet that Southern England had become 'The American 49th State'.

*

Although BOLERO was in full swing by the middle of 1942, it became increasingly obvious to the joint planners that an invasion into Europe through Northern France by either the end of 1942 or any time in 1943 was a non-starter. General Eisenhower, in his autobiography 'Crusade in Europe', noted at the time that any such expedition would have to be British-led with only American support. Moreover, the Allies had an insufficient number of naval vessels to actually land troops onto defended beaches, nor the aircraft to support them once ashore. Finally, there were still doubts about the logistic requirement to support such an operation, especially after the initial landings.

THE ALLIED JOINT CHIEFS MEETING IN WASHINGTON DC.
(US NAVAL HISTORY & HERITAGE COMMAND)

These realisations came to a head in mid-1942 after the halting of Rommel by the new 8th Army Commander, General Montgomery. Churchill in particular, had always harboured the view that it was the Empire fighting the Axis, not just the British. For him, the so-called 'jewel in the crown' of the Empire was India. This jewel was now under considerable threat, from both the East and the West. Success in North Africa allowed for shorter sea routes in the defence of India and a potential Allied jumping-off point to assault Europe from the Mediterranean. Now, with the unlikely ability to launch ROUNDUP even in 1943, Churchill had the opportunity to reinforce North Africa.

The obvious necessity to postpone ROUNDUP presented the Americans with a dilemma. The 'Germany first' agreement had been at considerable expense to the American defence of the Pacific against the Japanese, especially for the US Navy still smarting after Pearl Harbour. More importantly, BOLERO had already delivered substantial troop numbers to the UK, including some 30,000 that were sitting relatively idle as garrison troops in Northern Ireland.

THE FIRST AMERICAN TROOPS TO ARRIVE IN THE UNITED KINGDOM WERE STATIONED IN
NORTHERN IRELAND AS GARRISON TROOPS, RELEASING BRITISH TROOPS FOR OPERATIONS
OVERSEAS. (US NATIONAL ARCHIVES & RECORDS ADMINISTRATION)

Having met again in Washington in May 1942, Roosevelt was persuaded by Churchill that, without the possibility of ROUNDUP in 1943, an invasion of North-West Africa would be – quite literally – better than nothing. Moreover, this was enthusiastically supported by Stalin who desperately needed Western pressure put on the Germans to draw troops away from the Eastern fronts.

Eisenhower recounted that the psychological impact on the Allies and within the occupied countries would be disastrous '... (if) positive action of some kind were not undertaken during 1942.' As a result, action was taken; on the 25th July 1942, Roosevelt signed an agreement with Churchill committing US troops to Operation TORCH, a series of simultaneous Allied landings onto beaches in Morocco and Algeria. Originally planned for the 7th October 1942 this was later postponed to 7th November. The American commander chosen was none other than General Eisenhower.

Operation TORCH and the subsequent successful outcome in North Africa in May 1943 led to the landings on Sicily in August 1943. With Italian support for continuing the war faltering, Mussolini's regime collapsed in September 1943 and Italy surrendered to the Allies. On the Eastern Front, the German Sixth Army surrendered at Stalingrad, paving a way for future Russian offensive operations.

With the strategic decision to open a Second Front in Northern France finally agreed, the operational decisions of how and exactly when continued to tax the planners. By as early as 1942, Allied senior commanders fought their campaigns as 'combined operations'. General Montgomery in particular proved in North Africa that an integrated force from all three services was the way forward. He also showed that there had to be sufficient logistic support in place. What Montgomery developed in Libya and Tunisia in 1942 and 1943 was proved in Sicily and Italy in 1943 and 1944. This would now be the principal for Operation OVERLORD.

2

PLANNING AND PREPARATION FOR THE SECOND FRONT

Back in July 1942, Admiral Sir Bertram Ramsey had published a survey entitled 'Provisional Assessment of Naval Implications of ROUNDUP, 1943'. Although Ramsey summarised that the British facilities were inadequate from which to mount an invasion, there was an enclosure entitled 'Preliminary Forecast of Assault Stations for Naval Forces and Shipping'. One decision agreed and adhered to until June 1944 was that British Forces would be built-up and launched from the South-East of the country while the Americans would launch from the South-West.

By 1942 Falmouth was a busy and bustling naval base under Plymouth Command. As with all Royal Navy shore bases – 'stone frigates' in naval parlance – Falmouth was named HMS Forte under an Admiral referred to as 'Flag-Officer-In-Charge' or FOIC. For much of the war this was a retired Admiral, Sir Bertram S. Thesiger, replaced in February 1944 by Admiral Sir Fredrick Edward-Collins, on relinquishing command of HMS Cormorant, the naval base at Gibraltar that covered the North Atlantic.

The ROUNDUP Administrative Planning Staff investigated the suggestion from one of its many sub-committees that the ports of Falmouth and Fowey should be looked at in detail for receiving US Forces and their stores during BOLERO. Subsequently, the UK Ministry of War Transport produced a report issued on 25th July 1942. In Falmouth they had inspected the then King's, Empire and Queen's jetties alongside the road and rail facilities. Their conclusions were enlightening. The final report stated that:

'In view of the present important use of the port and the limited rail facilities...Falmouth is not suitable...It might, however, be well regarded as a reserve port for use in an emergency when some temporary interference with ship repairs might have to be allowed.'

At Fowey they looked at No.8 jetty, then some 500ft long and purpose-built for the china-clay industry. It was, they noted, only able to accept cargo vessels drawing 25ft and who could discharge their own cargo. Rail facilities away from the harbour were good, but ran into a choke-point at Lostwithiel, as they did from Falmouth. Their conclusion was the same as that for Falmouth; of use but only in an emergency.

The size of the US in-load into the United Kingdom took many by surprise, as did the actual requirements to mount the three-divisional assault then planned for 1943. But emergency there was and the Lend-Lease programme had kicked in, as had Admiral Ramsey's survey.

On 7th October 1942, the same ROUNDUP planning staff noted that at Falmouth and Fowey '…improvements to the facilities at these ports are well in hand…'. In the same report, the staff noted that there would be a requirement for 70 Landing Ship (Tank) (LST) and 150 for the smaller Landing Craft (Tank) (LCT) loading points or 'hards'.

Initially it was British contractors who undertook the massive task of preparing the required facilities. With Falmouth and Fowey now being upgraded, locations for 'hards' were identified, primarily in Falmouth, along the River Fal, in the Helford River and on both banks of the River Tamar opposite Plymouth. Today these are well known, but back in 1942-1943 they were largely hewn out of new ground and their locations closely guarded. Each hard was given an identifying code. These and their locations in Cornwall were as follows:

PF-1	Polgerran Wood, River Fal	2 x LSTs
PF-2	Turnaware Point, River Fal	4 x LSTs
PF-3	Harvey's Yard, Falmouth	2 x LCTs
PF-4	Taylor's Garage, Falmouth	4 x LCTs
PH	Polgwydden (Trebah), Helford River	2 x LSTs
PP-1	Upper Barn Pool, Mt. Edgecombe	4 x LSTs
PP-3	Lower Barn Pool, Mt. Edgecombe	4 x LCTs
PS	Jupiter Point, Devonport	2 x LCTs

(Alongside all of the above, it was also proposed that the Prince of Wales' Pier, Falmouth, would also be used to embark troops onto Landing Craft Infantry (Large) (LCI(L)s)).

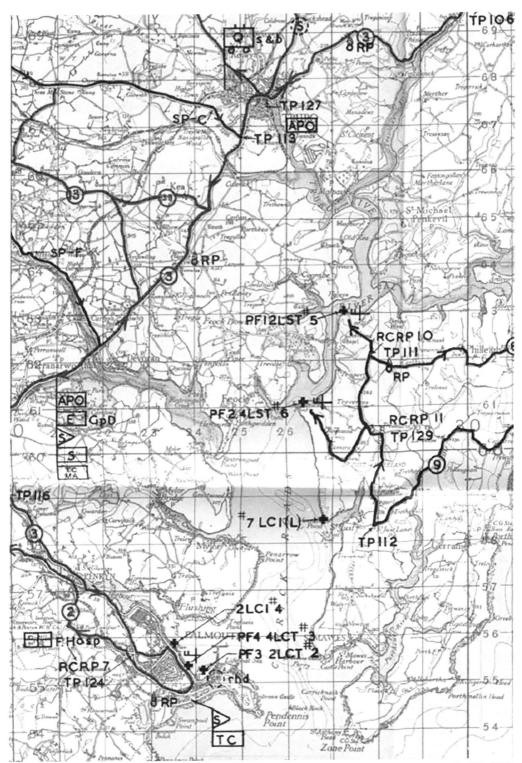

MAP – AN EXTRACT FROM THE OFFICIAL AMERICAN MAP OF THE FALMOUTH HARDS AND THE
ROUTES INTO AND OUT OF THEM, PUBLISHED BY SOUTHERN BASE SECTION.
(IKE SKELTON COMBINED ARMS RESEARCH LIBRARY)

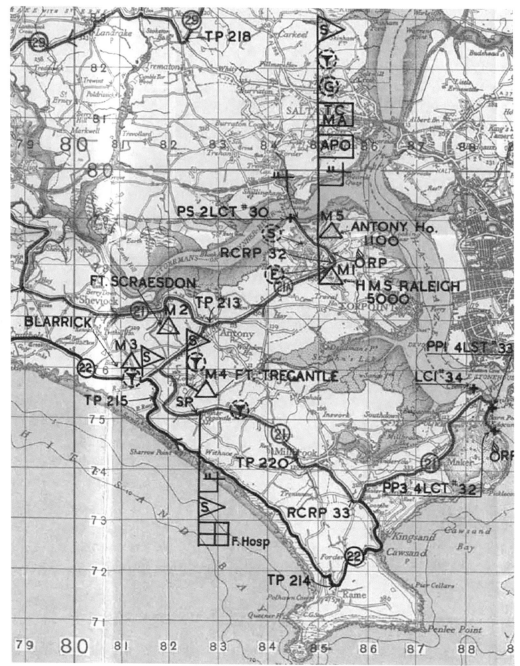

MAP –THE HARDS ON THE RAME PENINSULAR. (IKE SKELTON COMBINED ARMS RESEARCH LIBRARY)

The wartime biography of Bernard Breakell, a civilian Foreman of Works seconded to Falmouth by Plymouth Command, recalled that the building contract went to a London-based company 'Harbour and General Works Ltd'. They in turn recruited a large force of over 100 workmen to prepare the sites and the hard standings, or 'hards'.

These sloped gently into the water and covered the mean tide levels at both high and low water. LSTs and LCTs with their very shallow drafts were able to approach these points, lower their forward ramps and load or unload their cargos.

The hards themselves were made up of flexible concrete matting resembling a chocolate bar, mass produced in moulds and usually in a configuration of 3x5 'pads'. Soon large dumps of this matting were to be seen at the designated points on the Fal. Jutting out from the hards were temporary jetties, known as 'dolphins'. These were little more than steel piles driven into the river bed with wooden gangways attached. Each 'dolphin' also had a water pipe – and in some cases a fuel pipe – incorporated for immediate replenishment. These piers would allow vessels to tie up alongside prior to loading or unloading.

*

The American military's attitude to operational command was very different to that of the British. At higher levels, the Americans would draw up an outline plan and expect more junior commanders to add the details. The British were the opposite; the senior operational commanders would draw up the complete plan and expect the junior commands to carry it out. While both had their pros and cons, the American system of command allowed for immediate action once decided upon, but only so long as there were the adequate logistics to support it. Accordingly, while British contractors were putting in the hards on the River Fal, the first wave of the flood of the American military was arriving in Scotland. These were elements of the US Navy's Construction Battalions (CB), more often termed 'SeaBees'.

The CB founding-father was US Rear Admiral Ben Moreell. In 1942 he was the USN's Chief of Staff at the Bureau of Yards and Docks. He was determined to build a militarised naval construction force and in early January 1942 he received permission from the US Bureau of Navigation to form a 'construction regiment', composed of three 'construction battalions'. For manpower, Moreell approached the huge construction industry for volunteers. The first recruits came from the workforces of the huge American building programmes, such as the Boulder Dam in Colorado and those working on the skyscrapers in New York. In all during the war, some 175,000 were recruited, a fair few seeing service in Cornwall.

On 30th November 1942 the first elements of the 29th Construction Battalion arrived at US Base 2 in Rosneath, Scotland, relieving the 1,000-man civilian work-force – both British and American – that had yet to complete the build.

On 15th December 1942, the Admiralty informed C-in-C Plymouth that '…accommodations and berthing arrangements for assault conditions were required…by 1st July 1943, with 75 percent by 1st April 1943'. In turn Plymouth informed the navy commanders at Appledore, Dartmouth, Devenport and Falmouth that all unoccupied buildings were to be handed over first and only then should requisitioning of suitable occupied accommodation be sought.

REAR ADMIRAL BEN MOREELL – THE 'FATHER OF THE SEABEES'. HE WENT ON
TO BECOME A FULL ADMIRAL AFTER THE WAR.
(US NAVAL HISTORY & HERITAGE COMMAND)

For the Americans, however, there was a problem. Operation TORCH and the landings in Morocco and Algeria – often referred to as the 'Mediterranean Interlude' – had drained assets from the OVERLORD preparations. A pause was therefore required while additional assets were found elsewhere. This necessitated either a redoubling of the building and training programmes for naval craft and military manpower, or the diversion of logistics from other theatres, in either the Mediterranean or the Pacific. It would not be until May 1943, after the Washington Conference, that the Combined Chiefs of Staff gave the orders for the American build up in the United Kingdom to begin in earnest.

3

THE US NAVY ARRIVES
IN CORNWALL

T he maritime operation to land the Allies on the beaches in Northern France was Operation NEPTUNE and the American 'Western Task Force (WTF)' was to use the facilities of the Royal Navy's Plymouth and Portsmouth Commands. Overall American naval command in Europe (COMNAVEU) went to Admiral Harold Stark, commander of the US 12th Fleet. Upon him fell the responsibility of preparation for and receipt of the huge American maritime effort. He was to ensure the logistics were in place and the complete force – both naval and ground – was adequately trained and briefed for what lay ahead.

ADMIRAL HAROLD R. STARK USN – COMMANDER US NAVAL FORCES IN EUROPE (COMNAVEU). THIS PHOTOGRAPH IS PROBABLY TAKEN IN EARLY SUMMER 1943 IN THE ORKNEYS. (US NAVAL HISTORY & HERITAGE COMMAND)

Although Admiral Stark had ultimate responsibility for the US NEPTUNE Forces, it was decided that a number of subordinate commands within 12th Fleet would be responsible for differing areas of the operation. Principle amongst these was command of the new 'Task Force 122', the actual fleet for the landing force. Command of WTF fell to Rear Admiral Alan G Kirk, the former Commander of US Amphibious Forces, Atlantic Fleet. The former US Naval Attaché in London between 1939 and 1941, Kirk's primary task was to develop the detailed amphibious plan for NEPTUNE in London. As such, he was assigned an additional commander to oversee all the naval assets for the operation. Known as the 11th Amphibious Force, this was to be commanded by Rear Admiral John L. Hall who established his headquarters in Plymouth.

REAR ADMIRAL ALAN G. KIRK, USN. KIRK INITIALLY HAD TO DEVELOP US ORDERS FOR OPERATION NEPTUNE PRIOR TO SUBSEQUENTLY COMMANDING THE AMERICAN 'WESTERN TASK FORCE' OR TF-122. (US NAVAL HISTORY & HERITAGE COMMAND)

US REAR ADMIRAL JOHN L. HALL, COMMANDER OF THE US 11TH
AMPHIBIOUS FORCE AND SUBSEQUENTLY COMMANDER TASK FORCE
124 SEEN HERE ONBOARD US ANCON, HIS COMMAND SHIP ON 6TH
JUNE 1944. (US NAVAL HISTORY & HERITAGE COMMAND)

All along the South Coast, surveys had been completed and bases identified for future operations. In Cornwall the US Navy decided on Falmouth, St Mawes and Fowey. These were confirmed by the end of July 1943 and the agreements with the Royal Navy finalised. These would give the American Navy full freedom of action for command, organisation, training and support for their own forces. On the 28th July 1943, Admiral Stark informed the Navy Department in Washington that:

'...the British (are) to make available to us nearly all the housing, office and ship facilities that we need in Appledore, Falmouth, Fowey, Dartmouth, Salcombe, Teignmouth and Plymouth...the Royal Navy (will) supply...about 65% of naval stores, port machinery, boats, moorings etc, which we require. The requests on the United States for material (will be) kept to an absolute minimum'.

To ensure a suitable base and maintenance organisation, Admiral Stark sort authority to establish a 'craft and bases component' to his command. This was agreed and established as the 'Landing Craft and Bases, Europe' or LANCRABEU, sometimes referred to as 'LandCrab'. Another US Rear Admiral – John E. Wilkes – was appointed to command, becoming COMLANCRABEU for short. Wilkes reported for duty on the 1st September 1943 and immediately assumed command of all the US craft and port facilities that pertained to NEPTUNE. He established his headquarters initially in Falmouth on the 13th October 1943, before transferring this to Plymouth on the 3rd January 1944.

REAR ADMIRAL JOHN E. WILKES (L) WATCHES A DAWN EXERCISE AT WOOLACOMBE, THE AMERICAN AMPHIBIOUS LANDING SCHOOL, NORTH DEVON ON 31ST OCTOBER 1943. (US NAVAL HISTORY & HERITAGE COMMAND)

At this point, it is worth noting that by the 1st June 1943 there were already 22,000 US Navy personnel stationed in the United Kingdom. The majority of these were based on Plymouth Command with 8,000 in Plymouth itself, 3,000 at Falmouth and 2,000 at Dartmouth, where the Royal Naval College had been removed completely to the East Coast in December 1943 in order to make way for the Americans. In addition, the US Navy built its primary naval ordnance depot at Exeter that needed some 2,700 personnel to operate.

*

Back in Washington on the 24th August 1943, US Navy Reserve (USNR) Commander James E. Arnold visited the office of the Vice Chief of Naval Operations. He was ordered to recruit and equip a small force of 20 officers and 325 ratings and sail for the United

Kingdom. His unit was to be called 'FOXY-29' for the journey. Just prior to sailing from New York, Arnold was informed that he was to establish a US Naval Advanced Amphibious Base (USNAAB) at Falmouth, Cornwall. Under his administrative command, there were to be two sub-bases: one at St Mawes and another at Fowey. Prior to the main body of the base arriving from America, an advance party under the command of Commander L.B. Ard from COMNAVEU had taken up residence in Falmouth and were overseeing the building of a camp on Beacon Hill, described by the Americans as '...part grazing land and (part) swampland...'.

Prior to Commander Arnold arriving in Falmouth, two USN Advanced Amphibious Training Sub-Bases (USNAATSB) were established at St Mawes and Fowey, under base commanders Lieutenant Commanders Frank A. Varney and John P. Beale respectively. Their roles were to establish, train and then operate two landing craft Flotillas, known as 'Standing Landing Craft Units' (SLCU) using the small Landing Craft, Vehicle (Personnel) (LCV(P)s and Landing Craft, Mechanised (LCM)s. These boats had a crew of four and were able to transport some 30 soldiers apiece, although the LCMs were also able to carry a medium tank. These craft were to be used in the final run-ups to the beaches in the initial waves of any landing. St Mawes was to host SLCU-2 and Fowey SLCU-7.

COMMANDER JAMES E. ARNOLD (USNR) AT HIS DESK IN THE HYDRO HOTEL, FALMOUTH. (US NATIONAL ARCHIVES & RECORDS ADMINISTRATION)

US LANDING CRAFT VEHICLE (PERSONNEL) (LCV(P)) COME ASHORE AT SLAPTON SANDS. THESE
VESSELS ARE THOUGHT TO HAVE BEEN EITHER FROM ST MAWES OR FOWEY.
(US NAVAL HISTORY & HERITAGE COMMAND)

A LANDING CRAFT MECHANISED (LCM) EVACUATES LIGHTLY WOUNDED TROOPS FROM THE
BEACHES IN NORMANDY, 6TH JUNE 1944. (US NAVAL HISTORY & HERITAGE COMMAND)

The first problems to overcome were with accommodation. Although the Royal Navy's Plymouth Command anticipated large numbers of US servicemen, they had no idea just how many would be sent. Initial arrivals at all three bases went into the existing hotels and private houses. This was not as difficult as it first seemed due to the restrictions in the Southern coastal belt. The Government banned indiscriminate travel in and out for some months either side of D-Day, freeing up the majority of the hotel rooms.

In Falmouth, the US Navy initially established its headquarters in The Greenbank Hotel, later moving it across the road to 4 Stratton Place. As personnel numbers increased, American officers remained billeted in The Greenbank Hotel, with the NCOs and Ratings using the King's Hotel, close to the Prince of Wales' Pier. In addition the Falmouth Hotel, Cliff Road and St Michaels Hotel on Stracey Road were also requisitioned. The former was used to house senior American officers and the finance office. The latter was taken over as the American base hospital and dispensary. At the time, it was described as '…an up-to-date building with central heating, spacious grounds and excellent location'.

In St Mawes and Fowey, hotel accommodation and private houses were also used to begin with, although the official history of USNAATSB St Mawes revealed an odd twist to the tale. The Idle Rocks Hotel and the Ship & Castle Hotel were used for the enlisted men while the officers were given the private houses Carricknath and Penmore. On arriving,

'…all hands were immediately restricted to their quarters for a 48-hour period for the primary purpose of cleaning, fumigating and squaring-away (their) living quarters. The restriction made a remarkable impression on curious civilians, who were surprised to find that American sailors were not wholly undisciplined'.

The offices for the Officer Commanding and his deputy were established in Carricknath, while the base was established at the then Bird's Boat Yard on the River Percuil.

LIEUTENANT COMMANDER DWIGHT SHEPLER, AN AMERICAN NAVY WAR ARTIST, SKETCHING, PROBABLY AT GROVE PLACE, FALMOUTH. SHEPLER WAS INITIALLY POSTED TO USNAAB FALMOUTH IN ORDER TO RECORD THE AMERICAN PRE-INVASION BUILD-UP TO D-DAY. ON THE 6TH JUNE, 1944, HE LANDED ON ONE OF THE OMAHA BEACHES. (US NAVAL HISTORY & HERITAGE COMMAND)

LCV(P)s OF SLCU-2 IN
ST MAWES HARBOUR AS
PAINTED BY LIEUTENANT
COMMANDER SHEPLER IN 1944.
(US NATIONAL ARCHIVES &
RECORDS ADMINISTRATION-
SHEPLER)

In Fowey, the Americans had another role alongside just providing a trained landing craft flotilla. They were also expected to provide facilities for naval craft on their way to Plymouth, many of whom would have recently crossed the Atlantic or made their way South from Londonderry or Rosneath. The Hotel Fowey, as well as St Catherine, Penlee, Greenbank and Dagland's were requisitioned. Alongside these, the private houses at Carnethic and Mixtow House also went to the Americans.

ABOVE: A LARGE QUONSET HUT USED FOR REPAIRING BOTH AMERICAN AND BRITISH LCMs AND LCV(P)S AT GROVE PLACE, FALMOUTH. (ROYAL CORNWALL POLYTECHNIC SOCIETY, FALMOUTH HISTORY ARCHIVE)

LEFT: FOLLOWING ON FROM OPERATION TORCH, LST-325 ENTERS DRY DOCK AT FALMOUTH IN DECEMBER 1943. AFTER D-DAY, FALMOUTH DOCKS WERE ALMOST EXCLUSIVELY TURNED OVER TO SHIP REPAIR. (US NAVAL HISTORY & HERITAGE COMMAND)

'...AND THEY ENTERED TWO BY TWO...' — THE SHEER SIZE OF THE DRY DOCKS AT FALMOUTH
MADE THEM IDEAL FOR FAST SHIP REPAIR. HERE LSTs-325 AND 356 IN DRY DOCK AT FALMOUTH
DURING DECEMBER 1943 FOLLOWING ARRIVAL FROM NORTH AFRICA.
(US NAVAL HISTORY & HERITAGE COMMAND)

NOTHING MUCH HAS CHANGED...FOWEY PLACE AND THE CHURCH OF ST. FIMBARRUS ABOVE
THE RIVER PACKED WITH US NAVY LANDING CRAFT AS PAINTED BY LIEUTENANT COMMANDER
SHEPLER. (US NATIONAL ARCHIVES & RECORDS ADMINISTRATION-SHEPLER)

The harbours themselves also required considerable expansion. At Falmouth and Fowey, a large number of mooring lines needed to be provided for both large and small attack and landing craft alike. In Plymouth Command the initial requirement was estimated to be 1,100 moorings and a similar number of berths, both at anchor and alongside.

It was also anticipated that there would be a considerable requirement for both general and battle repair of vessels. The four Silley and Cox dry docks at Falmouth were ideal for major repairs and would be used extensively for the last two years of the war. For the smaller craft the US Navy took over Grove Place in Falmouth. Here they established a small maintenance base with a stores complex. In St Mawes, Bird's Yard was taken over and at Fowey a new complex was built from scratch on the beach below Mixtow House.

Alongside some of these smaller bases – at Falmouth, Mylor and Fowey – a series of simple low concrete piers evenly spaced twelve feet apart were constructed, the first two locations by E. Thomas and Son. Known as 'grids', these piers were set into the beach midway between high and low water. They worked by floating the flat-bottomed landing craft – anything from the smaller LCV(P)s to the larger LCTs – over the piers and securing them there until left high and dry by the receding tide.

Interestingly, the American military were not new to the area around Fowey. Back in the 'ROUNDUP' planning days, Headquarters Southern Command at Wilton had been willing to offer the Americans land on which to establish two major ammunition dumps. They suggested an area from the North of Launceston, South to Fowey. Although Fowey Harbour itself had been rejected as a storage depot, it was considered suitable for the in-load of stores, largely due to the single track railway line that ran directly from Lostwithiel to the eight China Clay jetties in Fowey Harbour. The ammunition was to be moved from Fowey Harbour to the depots using the railway while all road transport would have to use roads that had been widened. As always, the problem would be accommodation with some 2,000 beds required in the local area. The first depot – O-655 – was to be located between Lostwithiel and Liskeard and able to house some 36,000 tons. Somewhat confusingly it was to be called 'Fowey Ammunition Depot'. The second depot – O-666 – was to be even larger and established North of Launceston to hold some 50,000 tons. Both were to have opened on the 1st October 1942, but Operation TORCH intervened... .

*

Within the somewhat ad hoc American system, SLCU-2 was the first US Navy NEPTUNE unit to arrive in Cornwall, establishing itself in St Mawes on 17th August 1943. Under the command of Lieutenant (jg) Paul J. Raab, the Flotilla was formerly commissioned into service on the 7th September. The unit itself consisted of 20 officers and 60 four-man boat crews, a total of 240 NCOs and ratings. Alongside the SLCU, there were an additional 67 administrative and 'commissionary' (NAAFI) staff. This included a Red Cross shop that occupied the upper floors of the waterfront garage, today the St Mawes Gig Club and Village History Society. Initially the base only manned 18 LVC(P)s and six LCMs but almost immediately these were operating in ship to shore training onto Pendower Beach in Gerrans Bay.

For SLCU-7 in Fowey, things were more complicated in that there was no accommodation ready for them. After an initial review by Lieutenant (jg) Heminway Merriman on behalf of COMNAVEU on the 24th August 1943, a detachment of the US Navy's 29th Construction Battalion arrived on the 16th September to start converting the hotels and houses to the improved standards required by the Americans. Soon after, and prior to SLCU-7, a naval maintenance and repair unit (known as an 'E-10' team) occupied Mixtow House. USNAATSB Fowey went on to be commissioned on the 25th October and it was only then that SLCU-7, codenamed 'AJEP-29', arrived in Fowey on the 3rd November 1943. The Flotilla consisted of some 21 Officers and 225 NCOs and Ratings under the command of Lieutenant Wilton Wenker. Initially only six landing craft were provided and these were sailed in from Plymouth. Akin to SLCU-2, training started almost immediately, using Crinnis and Pentuan beaches for small-boat training. Their first exercise – 'Operation No.1' – was held on the 7th November, only four days after the Flotilla's arrival at its new base.

*

USNAAB Falmouth and its two sub-bases at St Mawes and Fowey required major construction work undertaken to complete the new bases, especially the accommodation.

Although detachments of the 29th CB had been at work since mid-September upgrading requisitioned civilian buildings, it would be the 81st CB that would make itself at home in all three Cornish bases. The battalion arrived in the United Kingdom in two tranches, being complete by the 5th October 1943, when it sent detachments down to Cornwall to relieve the 29th CB. Soon after, in November the battalion headquarters moved from Rosneath down to Penarth in South Wales where it was detailed to provide detachments all over the South-West.

Alongside the Cornish bases, work was undertaken in Penarth itself, as well as Milford Haven, Bicester, Salcombe, Dartmouth, Plymouth and Heathfield.

In Cornwall the work undertaken was impressive and is best summed up thus:

Falmouth	*Built two 750-man hutted camps.*
	Erected one 1,000-man tented camp.
	Converted St Michael's Hotel into a hospital.
St Mawes	*Built one 264-man hutted camp for USN Ratings.*
	Upgraded twelve civilian buildings, including two hotels.
Fowey	*Built a 1,000-man hutted camp.*
	Built a separate 500-man hutted camp.
	Built a 150-bed hospital.

The detachments of the 81st CB would remain in the Falmouth area until D-Day as they were re-rolled prior to the invasion. That said, while the US Navy trained, the CBs continued to work on the camps. In the end, they would spend four months working in Fowey and five months in both Falmouth and St Mawes.

*

With their camps being built around them, the American Navy got down to the task in hand. On the 13th October 1943, USNAAB Falmouth was officially commissioned and given the specific task of ensuring that the navy afloat was totally cared for. The men and their craft whose role was to transport the landing forces across to Northern France were to want for nothing. Training programmes were organised, catering for all, from individual ratings all the way up to complete Flotillas of LSTs or LCTs that were based on the harbour. Alongside all of this, Falmouth was also a major way point for individual vessels making their way to other South Coast ports, be they from the United States, the Mediterranean or just down from the bases in Londonderry or Rosneath. For the Americans, all of this had to be achieved in a very short time, from scratch and with the complete agreement of the Royal Navy's Plymouth Command. Contemporary American reports and accounts openly admit this was not necessarily easy.

Cornwall was – and still is – not that blessed with an easy road and rail network. The narrow roads and high Cornish hedges were not conducive to large vehicles and constant convoy movement. The rail network, especially the branch lines, tended to be single track and the bridges low. For all their supplies, USNAAB Falmouth had to rely on the main naval depot built at Exeter.

The Falmouth base history written in October 1944 noted two other problems. First, was the '…impractical landscape of the average English town…there was very little centralization…'. The report went on to note that it was two miles from the naval camp at Beacon Hill down to the main maintenance base at Grove Place or the new Headquarters in the Hydro Hotel. Second, the USNAAB command had also to act as a reception base. This was, in due course, to become very difficult barely three months before the invasion.

On the 28th October 1943 LST 30 arrived at Falmouth for repairs having crossed the Atlantic. Loaded on her upper deck was LCT 527. Four days later before both FOIC Falmouth and the Chief of Staff, COMLANCRABEU, LCT 527 was slid off into the harbour just as eight Landing Craft Infantry (Large) (LCI(L)) arrived from the United States a day early. These vessels were the first of their types to arrive in Falmouth for the invasion. There would be many, many more to follow.

*

As with Falmouth, the American training sub-bases at St Mawes and Fowey expanded rapidly. St Mawes was over crowded almost immediately the Americans arrived there, with 70 Officers and 596 NCOs and ratings 'on board' and by the end of January 1944, they were manning some 41 LCV(P)s and 38 LCMs. Such a large fleet necessitated that Bird's Yard had to be extended into a sizeable boat maintenance and repair facility. Initially a local contractor had built a steel re-fuelling and mooring pier but then a detachment of the 81st CB was ordered in to sizeably extend the yard.

Their efforts are still visible today; large concrete sea walls were built on the shingle beach and back-filling produced a sizable hard-standing. Etched into the top of one of the concrete walls by one of the CBs are the words '81st "SeaBees" Construction Battalion', proud testament to those hectic days.

AN LCT PIGGY-BACKED ON AN LST AT PLYMOUTH PRIOR TO BEING RE-LAUNCHED, SPRING 1943.
(US NAVAL HISTORY & HERTIAGE COMMAND)

THE LCT (6) IS SLID OFF THE DECK OF ITS LST CARRIER - PLYMOUTH, SPRING 1944.
(US NAVAL HISTORY & HERTIAGE COMMAND)

In addition to all the requisitioned hotels and houses, the 'SeaBees' were detailed off in St Mawes to build a 200-bed hutted camp. The Americans chose a vacant field in front of a house called 'Varth' high up on the point across today's Freshwater Lane. This in itself was not without problems, as the unit war diary recounts:

'The owner, a local lady, owned a sizable home and grounds across the road from the field. Her annoyance with the use of her land became one of the traditions of the base. Her objections were not so much to the despoiling of the land as to the fact that the structures interfered with her view of the Percuil River. So far as she was concerned her view was much more important than the progress of the war'.

Interestingly, slightly down-stream and on the opposite bank of the Percuil River was a British landing-craft training base. Using the British version of the LCM – the LCA – this base was located at Place. Requisitioned at the beginning of the war, the main house was initially used by the a heavy anti-aircraft battery located mid-way between Place and St Anthony's Coastal Battery.

Details are sparse but it would appear that this small base was a Combined Operations Training Base and was certainly in existence between July 1943 and June 1944. In a letter from FOIC Falmouth to Plymouth Command, it was noted that the Americans did not require Place as a maintenance base for landing craft as this could all be carried out in Falmouth at Taylor's Garage, adjacent to the hard at PF-4. In the same letter FOIC Falmouth asked if it were still required to erect six 'Robin Huts' for 36 minor landing craft, an additional four Nissen Huts for a workshop, the concreting of the lawns in front of the main house and installing heavy winches with which to haul the landing craft out of the water for cleaning or repair.

A POST-WAR PHOTOGRAPH OF PLACE HOUSE, ST ANTHONY IN ROSELAND WITH ITS SIX NISSEN HUTS. AFTER THE WAR, THESE WERE PUT TO A VARIETY OF USES INCLUDING ACCOMMODATION FOR RAMBLERS WALKING THE COASTAL PATH. (UNKNOWN PHOTOGRAPHER)

At Fowey, as with St Mawes, the American requirements grew. Prior to the invasion, Fowey also became a naval training establishment. This came about after the first major exercise to test combined landing operations. SLCU-7 provided 24 LCV(P)s and 9 LCMs for Exercise DUCK I that landed on the live fire ranges at Slapton Sands up the coast in Devon. This did not go well and it was decided that a serious amount of classroom instruction was required in all aspects of amphibious operations before further exercises were held. For the next few months, a vast array of both Army and Naval units went through the ad hoc schooling. Alongside this programme, additional instruction was given to both the landing craft Flotilla and other small craft units in 'ship-to-shore' operations. This included instruction in handling palletised cargo and loose stores from LCTs alongside casualty evacuation.

In addition to the naval training at Fowey, it was also decided to establish a 'Hospital Corps Training School' on behalf of USNAAB Falmouth. This was based in the huge 700-man 'recreation hut' while adjacent huts were used to quarter the 'corpsmen'. Any officers attending were separately housed in the requisitioned Greenbank Hotel (in Fowey). Such a facility was required as many of the LST and LCT crews had yet to see action and had very little idea what was before them. Ultimately, 150 officers and 2,850 hospital corpsmen would undertake the medical crash course and likely will have gone on to save many lives.

4

ONE LAST STRAW

On the 12th February 1944 General Dwight D. Eisenhower as the Supreme Commander, Allied Expeditionary Force was formally given his orders, a section of which read:

'You will enter the Continent of Europe and, in conjunction with the other United Nations, undertake operations aimed at the heart of Germany and the destruction of her armed forces. The date for entering the Continent is the month of May, 1944...'.

The supreme allied force given the role of undertaking the invasion was to be 21st Army Group, formed in July 1943. Alongside the ground command, it would also have a joint responsibility with both the Allied Naval Command and the Allied Expeditionary Air Force. Initially, the Army Group Commander was General Sir Bernard Paget, previously the Commander-in-Chief Home Forces. General Paget, however, was replaced by General Montgomery in the reshuffle following the appointment of General Eisenhower to the supreme command.

Eisenhower was very aware of the detailed COSSAC planning and was not happy with it. In his view '...the scale on which OVERLORD was being planned was too small and the front to be attacked was too narrow...'. Prior to flying to America to discuss his new command in Washington, Eisenhower had confided his worries with both Montgomery and his deputy General Bedell Smith. He went on to instruct them to examine the plans carefully and consider revisions. Interestingly, both men also discussed these worries with Winston Churchill who had been recovering from pneumonia in Marrakesh after the Cairo and Tehran conferences. He too agreed that the attack was on too narrow a front and did not include the capture of a major port to support future stores supplies to the forces already ashore.

Montgomery arrived back in the United Kingdom on the 2nd of January 1944 and Eisenhower on the 15th. A week later, the latter held his first command conference at which changes to the OVERLORD plan were discussed in detail. The three-division attack was to be increased to five and the frontage area doubled from twenty-five to fifty miles. The latter was to include a landing on the Cotentin Peninsular to possibly facilitate the early capture of the port at Cherbourg. Such an increase in forces would also require eight additional fighter squadrons, alongside 200 additional troop-carrier aircraft for an additional parachute division that was to be included.

Naval forces would also need to be considerably increased. Initial planning had worked on the premise that the Royal Navy was to have provided the majority of the supporting vessels. With two additional naval task forces required for the additional divisional assaults, this would be most difficult. It would require withdrawing Atlantic convoy protection, stopping the escort of reinforcements going to the Far East and removing naval support to the Italian campaign. To add to the difficulties, there was also an acute shortage of landing craft.

The Royal Navy had already postponed the completion of nineteen major projects in order to construct 75 additional LCTs with an additional 70,000 untrained workers moved into the shipyards to do so. Without additional American naval support, OVERLORD would have been largely impossible as a five-division assault.

After much wrangling between London and Washington, agreements were reached that relied on '…two cardinal variations of the Allies' plans…'. The first was the postponement of the landings from the 1st May back to the 31st. The second was more difficult and involved the possibility that Operation ANVIL, the proposed landings in the South of France, might be delayed in order to allow dedicated naval craft to be transferred to the Channel.

The revamping of the Allied plan for OVERLORD had a profound effect on Cornwall and its involvement with the future 'Second Front'. Up until the middle of 1943, the county had primarily been involved in supporting and training elements of the US Navy. Now there was an urgent need to base assault troops and corresponding numbers of Service of Supply units in the county who would support them in their preparations.

GENERAL DWIGHT D. EISENHOWER AND HIS JOINT COMMAND — FEBRUARY 1944. LEFT TO RIGHT: LIEUTENANT GENERAL OMAR BRADLEY, ADMIRAL SIR BERTRAM H. RAMSAY, SIR ARTHUR W. TEDDER, GENERAL DWIGHT D. EISENHOWER, GENERAL SIR BERNARD MONTGOMERY, SIR TRAFFORD LEIGH–MALLORY, LIEUTENANT GENERAL WALTER BEDELL SMITH. (IMPERIAL WAR MUSEUM)

5

THE WESTERN TASK FORCE
AND AMERICAN LANDING FORCES

The Western Task Force – TF-122 – was the American naval force that would land the American 1st Army on the beaches in Normandy. TF-122 comprised some 2,010 vessels of all sizes, commanded by Rear Admiral Alan G. Kirk USN. TF-122 was itself sub-divided with Task Force 124 (TF-124) delivering troops to the Omaha beaches and Task Force 125 (TF-125) delivering to the Utah beaches. The immediate support to the two assault forces was Follow-Up Force B, also known as Task Force-126 (TF-126).

The American 1st Army was sub-divided by corps with V Corps assaulting Omaha and VII Corps landing on Utah. The former primarily consisted of the 1st, 2nd and 29th Infantry Divisions and the latter had the 4th, 9th, 79th and 90th Infantry Divisions under command. Alongside the assaulting infantry, a vast force of supporting arms, beach units and logistics were also going to land. Principal among these were the Engineer Special Brigade (ESB) groups. The 1st ESB was to land on Utah Beach and the 5th and 6th ESB to land on Omaha. These brigades included specialist beach battalions to receive and direct the follow-on forces, USN demolition teams to remove the beach obstacles, engineers to open the exists off the beach and the like. What the Americans did not have with them were specialised armoured units such as the 'Armoured Vehicle Royal Engineers' (AVRE) to suppress fortifications, the Sherman 'Crab' flail tanks to beat a path through a minefield and vehicle-born bridges to cross any anti-tank ditches encountered. They were offered such vehicles by the British but in the end only chose to use 'Duplex Drive (DD)' swimming tanks, the vast majority of which sank in the rough seas before they could land.

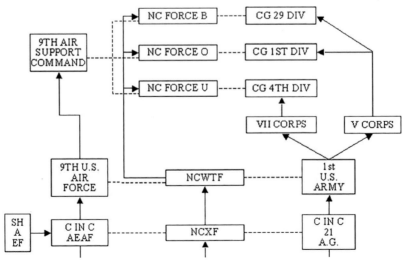

CHART – THE FINAL AMERICAN ORGANISATION FOR D-DAY. THE ADDITION OF AN AMERICAN INFANTRY AND AIRBORNE DIVISION ONTO THE CONTENTIN PENINSULAR POSTPONED THE INVASION BY A MONTH BUT SAVED MANY AMERICAN LIVES. (US NAVAL HISTORY & HERTIAGE COMMAND)

One of the first American divisions to arrive in the United Kingdom had been the 29th Infantry Division. The division was a National Guard unit and could trace its history back to the mid-eighteenth century. In the American Civil War some of the original constituent units belonged to either Union or Confederate Forces. This is very much reflected in the divisional 'ying-yang' badge of dark blue and grey. The division had previously seen action in World War 1 when it was called up and shipped to France to fight in the Meuse-Argonne region in 1918.

On the 3rd February 1941, the entire US National Guard was 'federalised', called-up, some ten months before the Japanese attack against Pearl Harbour. As such, the 29th was also one of the first divisions to move to the United Kingdom under Operation BOLERO, being preceded by the 1st Infantry, a regular division. On the 26th September 1942 the 29th Division was shipped to the United Kingdom crossing the Atlantic on the RMS Queen Mary. The journey was not without incident. HMS Curacao, sent out to escort them through British waters to Rosneath, misjudged a turn in front of the liner and was hit amidships. Cut clean in two, she sank immediately taking 332 of her crew with her.

NOT WITHOUT INCIDENT, THE RSM QUEEN MARY TRANSPORTED THE 29TH INFANTRY DIVISION TO THE UNITED KINGDOM, COLLIDING WITH AND SINKING HMS CURACAO. (US NAVAL HISTORY & HERITAGE COMMAND)

The Division was initially quartered in Tidworth, Wiltshire, on the edge of Salisbury Plain. Training began immediately but after eight months in Wiltshire, the 29th Division moved South to Devon and Cornwall, arriving in June 1943. This move was also unusual. Such was the training regime within the division under their commanding officer Major General Leonard T. Gerow that they largely marched themselves to the new headquarters at Tavistock and beyond. This was done as the British units they were replacing were coming in the opposite direction.

At that time, the 29th Infantry Division was composed of three infantry regiments, the 115th (1st Maryland), the 116th (The Stonewall Brigade) and the 175th (5th Maryland). In turn, each regiment was composed of three battalions, each composed of four rifle companies. In all, an American regiment would number 3,118 men, with 871 in each of the battalions and 193 men in each of the companies. The divisional organisation also included artillery, engineer, ordnance and medical units likewise reflected in both the regiments and the battalions where there were also detachments including administrative, medical and quartermaster personnel. In action, each regiment would form a combined arms Regimental Combat Team (RCT). For the 29th Division, these would be 115th, 116th and 175th RCTs.

Unlike the 1st Division, the 29th Division was not selected for operations in North Africa under Operation TORCH, remaining in Britain until June 1944. Indeed, the Division spent so much time in the United Kingdom that they were nicknamed 'England's Own'. Ultimately, the two divisions would work very closely together. On D-Day, 116th RCT landed on Omaha Beach under command of the 1st Infantry Division.

In moving down to the South-West at the beginning of June 1943, the majority of the 29th Division were stationed in Cornwall. The locations for the larger units in October 1943 were noted as follows, less 116th RCT that was under command the 1st Infantry Division for the landings:

Headquarters, 115th Regiment	*Bodmin*
1st Battalion, 115th Regiment	*St Austell*
2nd Battalion, 115th Regiment	*Scorne Cross, Launceston*
3rd Battalion, 115th Regiment	*Bodmin*
Headquarters, 175th Regiment	*Pendarves Estate, Camborne*
1st Battalion, 175th Regiment	*St Ives*
2nd Battalion, 175th Regiment	*Helston*
3rd Battalion, 175th Regiment	*Penzance*
29th Reconnaissance Troop	*Fort Scraesdon*
A Company, 104th Medical Battalion	*Bodmin*
C Company, 104th Medical Battalion	*Clowence Estate, Camborne*
110th Field Artillery Battalion	*Bodmin*

In July 1943, the division received a new commander, Major General Charles Hunter Gerhardt. Flown straight in from the United States, General Gerhardt had been commanding the recently-raised 91st Infantry Division in Oregon. Prior to his arrival in the West Country, a senior staff officer is claimed to have offered Gerhardt three pointers prior to his first senior command outside of America. He was advised that first, the 29th was likely to require serious amphibious training as it was undoubtedly to become involved in any future landings in Northern France. Second, the General was advised that he must be aware of Vicountess Astor living in Plymouth, a notable Virginian lady who not only had married into the British aristocracy on her second marriage but had also become a British Member of Parliament for the seat of Plymouth Sutton. And third, that the 29th were a National Guard division and that their discipline would unlikely be up to the standard of regular troops.

This latter point must have wrankled with Gerhardt '...a West Pointer, an old cavalryman and avid polo-player...a disciplinarian of the old school...'. Although General Gerhardt did not disappoint, his first order to his new division was to give them a three day holiday.

MAJOR GENERAL CHARLES H. GERHARDT TOOK COMMAND OF THE 29TH INFANTRY DIVISION IN JULY 1943, LEADING THEM ALL THE WAY TO GERMANY. (TAVISTOCK MUSEUM ARCHIVE)

In Cornwall it was found that Bodmin Moor was an ideal exchange for Salisbury Plain. There was plenty of freedom for soldiers to dig, vehicles to be driven and guns to be fired. At Berry Down, close to St Neot, artillery positions were established in order to fire onto the crags at Brown Willy, some seven miles away. In other areas, the remains of engine houses and their chimneys made excellent targets or, as with the Black Dog Shaft at Wheal Busy, Chacewater, an area for explosives demolition training. But it was on Dartmoor that the 29th Infantry Division did the majority of its training and nothing encompassed this more than General Gerhardt naming his personal Jeep 'Vixen Tor' after the largest mass of exposed granite between Princetown and Tavistock. This vehicle had to be immaculately turned out every hour of every day and would have to be cleaned out and washed up to four times each day by his driver.

GENERAL GERHARDT AND HIS JEEP 'VIXEN TOR'. (TAVISTOCK MUSEUM ARCHIVE)

As for Lady Astor, Gerhardt was charming and would always have the upper hand as he had access to fresh meat and vegetables. She would regale him and his senior officers with stories from her youth in Virginia or with local jokes. After Lady Astor took part in a divisional talent show, Gerhardt presented her with a pig painted head to toe in blue and grey, pertaining to one of her jokes. Besides the pig, Lady Astor was made an honorary private in the Division, rising to sergeant and ultimately becoming a second lieutenant by the end of the war.

*

Britain in war time was not a safe place. German bombing, the use of live ammunition on exercises, or even simply the black-out, all led to accidents. Many of these were fatal. The 29th Infantry had their fair share of them prior to D-Day. On the 23rd May 1943, six members of the 175th Infantry Regiment visited Bournemouth on leave from Tidworth. They had just checked in at the Metropole Hotel in the town centre when twenty-six Focke-Wulf 190 fighter-bombers raided the town just before 1.00pm, each with a single bomb. The raid killed 131, including the Americans. Twenty-two buildings were destroyed and a further thirty-seven were later demolished.

VICOUNT AND VICOUNTESS ASTOR PRIOR TO WORLD WAR 2. NANCY ASTOR STOOD FOR THE SEAT OF PLYMOUTH SUTTON AND WON, ENTERING PARLIAMENT IN 1919, THE FIRST WOMAN TO DO SO. SHE RELINQUISHED HER SEAT IN 1945. (US LIBRARY OF CONGRESS)

Exactly five months later, on the 23rd October, four members of the 110th Field Artillery Battalion based in the Duke of Cornwall's Light Infantry Regiment Depot in Bodmin were killed in action while serving with the Royal Navy. This unfortunately came about through a scheme devised by Headquarters V Corps to reward troops by sending them to gain operational experience with the Royal Navy. An officer, two NCOs and five Privates joined HMS Limbourne while others joined HMS Wensleydale. Both were part of the 15th Destroyer Flotilla, based out of Plymouth. On the night of the 22nd October, both vessels sailed for the Brittany coast on Operation TUNNEL, the hunt for the German blockade runner Munsterland, thought to be heading for Cherbourg. Unfortunately they ran into a German destroyer Flotilla that reacted more quickly and fired a barrage of torpedos. HMS Limborne was one of two ships hit, with her forward gun crew killed. It was here that the four American artillerymen had been stationed as ammunition handlers.

While the vast majority of Americans were polite, humble and more than appreciative of their lot in the United Kingdom, there were occasions that exposed a number of problems. Primary amongst these was the inherent racist attitudes of particularly the Southern-born white troops against any black SOS units. In 1942 there were only 12,000 African-American troops in the US Army, but this had risen to 130,000 by May 1944. Segregation was the order of the day with approximately 85% of white troops supporting it alongside only 48% of coloured troops. Unfortunately, the latter tended to be only allowed to have access to the more inferior facilities. An added problem was the attitude of the locals around the bases who saw no problems in seeing either black or white troops in their pubs, clubs and dances, infuriating a minority of the Americans.

SOS TROOPS WERE OFTEN AFRICAN–AMERICANS; FULLY ACCEPTED BY THE BRITISH BUT REJECTED BY A MINORITY OF US TROOPS. WITHOUT THEM, HOWEVER, SOS AND ITS OPERATION NEPTUNE LOGISTICS PLAN WOULD NOT HAVE GONE AS SMOOTHLY AS IT DID. (CRITICAL PAST)

This went right to the top, through General Eisenhower to President Roosevelt. Any number of orders were issued to try and quell the problems but they kept bubbling to the surface, on occasion leading to open street battles. In Launceston on the night of the 26th September 1943, a new SOS unit that included a large number of African-American troops were incensed when they were not allowed to drink in the same pubs as the white troops. Later that evening, a group of the former returned armed with an array of weaponry, including rifles and Tommy guns. A struggle ensured and two Military Policemen were wounded.

*

Any landing onto the beaches in Northern France would require serious co-operation of all the forces involved. Despite being fit and generally trained to use all their weapons and understand their tactics, the assault forces had also to digest the complex coordination and sheer difficulties of landing on an open beach with a live enemy. New weapons and new tactics had to be devised, practised and then integrated into what would become the largest operation of its time.

In July 1943, the Americans established an amphibious training centre on ten miles of beach and hinterland at Woolacombe, North Devon. Copies of the German concrete defences observed in Northern France were constructed, although this did not include beach obstacles as these had yet to appear across the Channel. Woolacombe was built to accept a complete regimental combat team, with the 116th RCT being the first through in September 1943. The course lasted three weeks.

US LCV(P)s LEAVE APPELDORE ON THEIR WAY TO THE BEACHES AT
THE WOOLACOMBE ASSAULT TRAINING CENTRE, LATE OCTOBER 1943.
(US NAVAL HISTORY & HERITAGE COMMAND)

In South Devon, the British Government went further. In October 1943 they requisitioned a long stretch of the coast between Strete and Torcross and all the farms inland up to a line between Blackawton and East Allington, in all some 30,000 acres. All residents and their livestock had six weeks to clear the area; 3,000 people and 180 farms. All village churches were carefully emptied of their artefacts, carvings and plate and their more precious architectural features were protected under sandbags. The pubs, of course, were cleared of all their remaining stocks of beer and cider. As the locals moved out, the American Army moved in and established a live-fire range. The selected area needed to be so large, in order to cater for rounds that ricocheted or, as sometimes happened, fired at the wrong range or off the wrong sighting scale.

A FAMILY LEAVES ITS COTTAGE TO MAKE WAY FOR THE ALLIED AMPHIBIOUS LIVE-FIRE AREA BASED ON SLAPTON SANDS. (US NAVAL HISTORY & HERITAGE COMMAND)

Slapton Sands had a number of useful similarities to what would likely be met on OMAHA, mostly of shingle over sand. The tidal range was fairly small, only 10 to 14ft, but enough to practise the US Navy in delivering troops by tides.

*

Prior to any exercise or operation there had to be some form of plan within which the assault troops could be marshalled into the correct order, for the correct ship and delivered at the correct time onto the correct beach. The foundation for such a plan was initially conceived by the British as far back as 1942 for Ops SLEDGEHAMMER and ROUNDUP, but by the middle of 1943 the American areas came under the planning control of XIX District, Southern Base Section. This was to be the 'Mounting Plan' in support of Operation NEPTUNE.

The British and the Americans agreed on three main points:

a. First, the initial assault waves onto the beaches must be as hard-hitting as possible. There would be no room for supporting troops and all such personnel would need to be stripped out and landed separately.

b. Second, the assaulting force needed to be composed of a varied number of experts in their specialist fields, not just 'bayonets'. Artillery observers, assault engineers, tanks, guns and the like would also need to be landed in well trained all-arms teams. They would need to be loaded onto the landing craft as they meant to get off.

c. Third, to achieve such aims, the assault force would require mustering and marshalling prior to moving to their embarkation hards for loading.

To ensure that such a plan worked, it was soon realised that the assault troops could not administer themselves. They would have to be looked after within comfortable, sanitary conditions with more than adequate facilities prior to moving onto their landing craft and ships within which they would be 'sealed' to ensure security. The next time they would disembark would be on the enemy coast. Such a plan necessitated one vital element: the date and time that the first waves would land. Everything else worked back from there.

The plan devised consisted of a number of phases through which the forces would flow. First was the home station phase, or the 'BOLERO installation' phase, as the Americans initially called it. These were the barracks or camps that were home to the troops. It was here that the units would shake themselves out, the administrative personnel would be detached from the assault troops and the latter would digest their initial movement orders; vehicles were to be waterproofed and last minute logistical problems sorted out.

Second were the 'marshalling areas'. It was here that all the tactical and operational necessities would be catered for. It was also here that each individual soldier was to be briefed on the actual assault plan. Security was paramount and thus each and every marshalling area was 'sealed', no one allowed out and no one allowed in. For the Americans, their own Military Police would cover the security within the marshalling area while the British police would cover the local civilian population. In all, the Americans would use 2,000 security personnel to patrol their camps.

Due to such tight security, every possible potential requirement that might be asked for was made available; food was plentiful, the beds comfortable, films and libraries laid on. Last letters and wills were written with the American postal units handling some 10,500 sacks of mail out of the camps and 13,000 sacks in. This included the final issue of any personal requirements – anything from a new rifle to a new razor. Weapons and vehicles were given a last check that included a final drive through deep water-filled pits in each area to check the waterproofing. It was also in these marshalling areas that each individual was issued with his life-belt, personal rations, additional ammunition and three prophylactics of which the majority ended up over personal watches, wallets and rifle muzzles. Each soldier was also issued 200 Francs in Allied invasion money, printed by the Allies to the everlasting fury of General de Gaulle. The American exchange rate was 2 US cents to the franc!

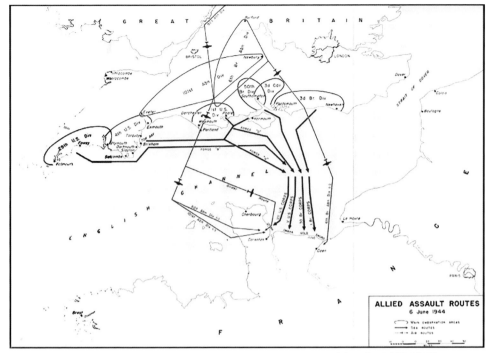

MAP – OPERATION NEPTUNE MARSHALLING AREAS AND THEIR CONVOY ROUTES TO NORMANDY. (THE HYPER TEXT HISTORIES)

A marshalling area also included a number of troop holding camps and railheads for vehicles and stores. Each area had a designation letter with the British having Camps 'A', 'B' and part of 'C' while the Americans had the other part of 'C', 'D' and 'K' to 'O'. In Cornwall, the US troops were marshalled in the majority part of 'M', located on the Cornish side of the Tamar opposite Plymouth and in areas 'N' and 'O'. These latter two areas were based on the embarkation hards around Falmouth and Helford.

THE INTERIOR OF PROBABLY ONE OF THE CAMPS WITHIN SAUSAGE 'O–D', RUNNING NORTH–EAST OUT OF HELSTON. (CRITICAL PAST)

These marshalling areas were administered by districts within the SnBS, in particular Districts XVIII and XIX. The commandant of the latter was Colonel Theodor Wyman Jr, a regular army engineer. He was tasked with providing suitable marshalling camps for the 29th Infantry Division and the assorted attached 1st Army assault troops. His plan was very simple – to take over many of the back roads and build the camps alongside these. The roads would provide the vehicle hard standings while in the adjacent fields temporary tented camps were erected. On a map, these long ribbon camps appeared as 'sausages' and hence they were all nicknamed 'sausage camps'. Some of these camps stretched a very long way, some over ten miles. Conversely, for 'M' Area, where many of the troops were based in large barracks with their embarkation points literally down the road, there was little need for 'sausage camps'.

AN AMERICAN JEEP FULLY LOADED AND WATERPROOFED FOR THE LANDINGS TRUNDLES PAST THE ENTRANCE TO A 'SAUSAGE CAMP'.

THE BOARD IN THE BACKGROUND APPEARS TO READ 'D-7', SUGGESTING THAT THIS IS ONE OF THE CAMPS OF 'O-D', LARGELY OCCUPIED BY ELEMENTS OF THE 175TH INFANTRY REGIMENT, 29TH INFANTRY DIVISION. (CRITICAL PAST)

AN AMERICAN 'SAUSAGE CAMP' IN CORNWALL. THE LENGTH OF THE FILM SEQUENCE SUGGESTS IT MIGHT BE CAMP 'F' OF MARSHALLING AREA 'O' BASED IN CHACEWATER, CORNWALL. (CRITICAL PAST)

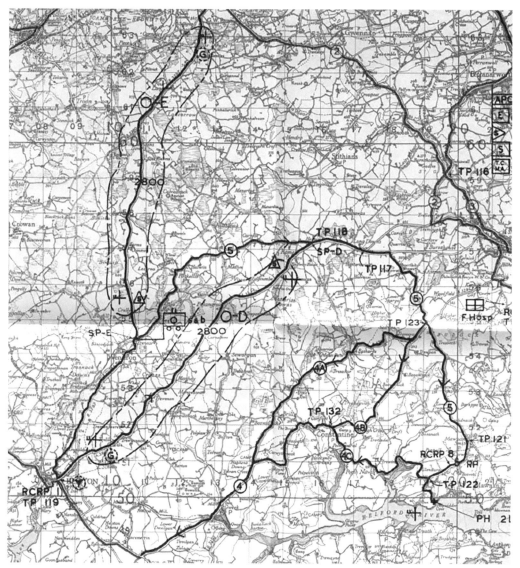

MAP – MARSHALLING CAMPS 'O-D' AND 'O-E' WERE BOTH LINKED TO THE EMBARKATION HARDS AT POLGWYDDEN (TREBAH) ON THE HELFORD RIVER. (IKE SKELTON COMBINED ARMS RESEARCH LIBRARY)

The final phase was embarkation. This was to begin on 'Load (L)-Day' and would be in direct relation to 'D-Day'. With everything and everyone ready to go, unit convoys would move down to the embarkation points. Every soldier and vehicle had a place earmarked on each individual landing craft. All vehicles would be driven – backwards – onto either the LCTs or LSTs while the general infantry would be shipped out to their LCI(L)s off-shore. In Falmouth, for instance, both the Prince of Wales's Pier and Massack Point, the latter close to the village of St Just-in-Roseland, were the infantry departure points.

TROOPS EMBARKING ONTO LCI(L)s AT THE PRINCE OF WALES PIER, FALMOUTH. THIS IS PROBABLY FOR EXERCISE DUCK I ON 30TH DECEMBER 1943. THE MAJORITY WEAR THEIR OVERCOATS AND CARRY THEIR BEDDING ROLES, ITEMS NOT CONDUCIVE TO STORMING A BEACH FOR REAL. (CRITICAL PAST)

Just as there was a detailed and intricate plan for the ground assault troops, there was a similar plan for the naval units and vessels that were to carry them. This plan was worked back from the designated time and place that each vessel was to land its troops and vehicles. There were a number of fixed parameters that could not be avoided – the mooring capacity of the ports and harbours for loading, vessels speeds in convoy and the minefields, both British and German. Thrown into the mix would be many unknowns, in particular the weather and the German reactions.

The plan devised outlined a number of phases for each landing craft. These worked on the premise that each vessel would move from its home port to its designated loading hard, load, move to its convoy forming-up point and finally, sail for Normandy.

A plan such as this covered many square miles and relied on the ability of the troops and their vehicles to move at the right time to the right point. As a result, the Americans established two huge road networks, one 16ft wide, the other 22ft wide; these roads were subsequently closed to all civilian traffic. Should any stretch of road not be of sufficient width, American engineers moved in and widened it. This was usually achieved by scraping back the verges and placing a layer of concrete over the top. Many of these patches are still visible today. Traffic was regulated and all one-way along particular routes. Virtually every cross-road or major turn had a traffic post and, in order to avoid any blockage, a large number of vehicle recovery and repair units were established throughout the network. Any vehicle that did breakdown was removed from the road and a replacement whistled up if it could not be repaired quickly.

US CONVOY ON A WIDENED CORNISH ROAD, LINED WITH AMMUNITION STORAGE BUNKERS JUST PRIOR TO D–DAY 1944. (CRITICAL PAST)

TRUCKS MOVE THROUGH MAWNAN SMITH UNDISTURBED. 'TP 121' STANDS FOR 'TRAFFIC POINT 121' AND WOULD BE HAVE BEEN MANNED BY THE AMERICAN FIELD SERVICE (AFS) STANDING IN THE ROAD. NOTE THE RED LION PUB AT THE TOP OF THE ROAD. (CRITICAL PAST)

6

EXERCISE, EXERCISE, EXERCISE

here are three basic tenets for military operations at all levels. The first states that any exercise or rehearsal for battle should be more gruelling, more difficult and perhaps more dangerous than the future action itself. The second states that any military plan will disintegrate on first contact with the enemy. And the third that time spent in reconnaissance is seldom wasted. Running into a series of large-scale exercises, the Americans fell foul of all three at some time or other, sometimes all three at once.

With the 'Mounting Plan' in place, all the planners were very keen to test it and iron out any problems. Although many of the troops were highly trained, large elements of the ultimate plan had yet to be tested. All of these would lead onto two major D-Day rehearsals, exercises FABIUS for the OMAHA landings and TIGER for those onto UTAH. This was particularly so with regards to the naval forces embarking troops and landing them, linking in the SLCUs at St Mawes and Fowey with the troop-carrying convoys and coordinating both the air and sea bombardments to cover the landings. With the establishment of the Woolacombe Assault Training Centre and the live-fire exercise and ranges at Slapton Sands, the time had now come to see what worked and what did not.

The first major exercise was written and planned in late 1943 to be undertaken in early January 1944. This was before both Eisenhower and Montgomery demanded the enlargement of the landing plan and before air reconnaissance began to note the growing obstacles that Rommel was putting onto the wide beaches in Normandy. This first exercise was called 'Exercise DUCK I'. Because of the firing of live ammunition and the security implications, the Americans deemed such exercises as 'operations'.

The first planning meeting for DUCK I was held on the 21st November 1943 and included representatives of US V Corps Headquarters, both the Royal and US Navies and relevant Service of Supply, Southern Base Section and XIX District representatives, all three alongside British representatives from both Southern Command and South-West District. The aim of this first foray was to practise the mounting of a landing, from concentration area to embarkation. Exercise control was with Headquarters XIX District and was broken down into two phases – the mounting and the landing. Royal Navy elements would provide real-time protection from both submarine and E-Boat attack and the IX US Air Force would provide protection in the air.

The first troops exercised in DUCK I were from the 175th Infantry Regiment and the 1st Engineer Special Brigade. With them went a number of headquarter teams, including one from the IX US Air Force and another from V Corps, both supported by the 56th Signal Battalion. The exercising troops were spread far and wide, from Helston to Taunton and embarkation was to take place in both Falmouth and Dartmouth. During the beach landing, some 10,242 men would be exercised and 1,096 vehicles of all types landed, with another 10,156 men from SnBS units employed to actually run the exercise.

As the troops left their concentration areas, they moved into temporary camps established in the Helston, Falmouth, Redruth, Truro and St Austell areas with another way to the East, at Lupton House near Dartmouth. These camps preceded the future marshalling areas that came later. Each area had fourteen tented camps and parking for 1,000 vehicles. The initial landing was planned for the 3rd January, 1944 but was delayed until the following day, the 4th.

US CONVOY CONTROL JEEP OF THE 29TH INFANTRY DIVISION PATIENTLY WAITS BEFORE BEING CALLED FORWARD TO EMBARK. SUGGESTED DATE IS DECEMBER 1943 DURING EXERCISE DUCK 1. (CRITICAL PAST)

ORDERS WERE ISSUED THAT ALL VEHICLES WERE TO REMAIN FULLY FUELED-UP AT ALL TIMES. (CRITICAL PAST)

Incorporated into DUCK I were a number of logistical tasks to be considered and tested. To move the considerable amount of stores that would be required to support the troops, four British coasters were pre-loaded in Bristol on the 24th December with ammunition, fuel and rations. These were 'skid-loaded' – palletised in today's parlance – for the first time.

Troops began moving into the marshalling areas on the 26th December and embarkation began on the 28th. In all, 14 LSTs, 26 LCTs and 23 LCI(L)s were used, supported by 5 LCMs and 151 LCV(P)s from both St Mawes and Fowey. Four British destroyers provided support and protection alongside several LCTs with 105mm field guns on the open vehicle decks.

EXERCISE DUCK 1. GLS OF THE 29TH INFANTRY DIVISION MARCH THROUGH FALMOUTH ON THEIR WAY FOR EMBARKATION. (CRITICAL PAST)

EXERCISE DUCK 1. GLS OF THE 29TH INFANTRY DIVISION MARCH DOWN THROUGH THE MOOR, FALMOUTH. (CRITICAL PAST)

The troops landed on the dot of 10.00am on the 4th January on Slapton Sands, but almost immediately things went array. Some naval craft came ashore in the wrong waves and the inshore ley caused problems for the troops moving inland as bridging failed to arrive on the beach on time. The Special Engineers landed twenty-five minutes after the assault troops and immediately began to clear the beach of mines as per their orders, but while other troops were landing. In the afternoon, the four British coasters arrived and their cargoes off-loaded into either one of the LCMs or into a DUKW, an amphibious truck. Throughout the time on the beach, the Americans tested any number of ideas from waterproofing of supplies, the skid-loads, track-laying and large tannoys with which to relay commands across the beach or out to sea. In all, the exercise lasted two days before all troops packed up and were returned to barracks by XIX District.

During the whole affair, there were any number of observers taking notes and seeing what was or was not working. The first exercise critique was held at V Corps Headquarters on the 12th January and at XIX Headquarters on the 20th and 26th. All agreed that DUCK I was a credible success as a first attempt. All agreed that the initial marshalling was excellent but there were any number of problems noted. One of the more worrisome threads running through the whole exercise was the obvious lack of tactical training displayed by the supporting troops landing behind the assault. This was especially so with the Special Engineers, whom many had actually participated in landings in Sicily and Italy during 1943. The average unloading time for the LSTs was ten hours, not the five required. Many also had incomplete manifests so that the beach masters had little idea what was in which ship.

LST-325 LANDS ELEMENTS OF THE 29TH INFANTRY ONTO SLAPTON SANDS, DEVON, DURING EXERCISE DUCK I HELD IN EARLY JANUARY 1944. (US NATIONAL ARCHIVES & RECORDS ADMINISTRATION)

DUCK I was quickly followed by DUCKs II and III. Importantly, a centralised exercise planning staff was established. DUCK II was planned for the 7th February with the landing to occur on the 14th and DUCK III from the 23rd February. The assault troops exercised would be the other two regimental combat teams of the 29th Infantry Division and those elements of the 1st Engineer Special Brigade (ESB) that were not present on DUCK I. As it was, the latter did not operate with the 29th Infantry on D-Day, being swapped for the 6th ESB. This was to have dire consequences for the 1st ESB, as will be seen later.

Interestingly, the DUCK series of exercises were tests of procedures, not rehearsals for the actual landing. Also, the fall-out from the addition of another assault division had yet to be felt and would most certainly cause further headaches for the planners. As such, the first true NEPTUNE rehearsal was Exercise FOX that was in itself a rehearsal for Exercise FABIUS I, itself the full rehearsal for the eventual OMAHA landings.

Although FOX was ordered by V Corps again, the mounting was undertaken by XVIII District, using totally new personnel and marshalling areas. The exercise landed on Slapton Sands on the 9th March and saw the 16th RCT of the 1st Infantry Division (the famous 'Big Red One') landing alongside the 116th RCT of the 29th Division as they were to do for real. A provisional Engineer Special Brigade Group landed behind them. As this was a XVIII District exercise, marshalling was undertaken in Dorset with embarkation at Plymouth, Weymouth, Dartmouth and Portland harbours. In all 16,923 troops were marshalled with 1908 vehicles.

LOADING LCT-209 WITH A GRANT ARMOURED RECOVERY VEHICLE AT TAYLOR'S YARD,
FALMOUTH, DECEMBER 1943. (US NAVAL HISTORY & HERITAGE COMMAND)

*

All across the South Coast, in Wales, even in Scotland and Northern Ireland, the Americans conducted exercises and experiments to work out the best methods for concentrating, marshalling, embarking and sailing Operation NEPTUNE. Death and injury were constant companions in these exercises but never more so than on the night of the 27th-28th April 1944.

Exercise TIGER was the UTAH Beach equivalent of FOX, a rehearsal of a rehearsal. The overall Anval commander was Rear Admiral Don P. Moon and the American 4th Infantry Division was the major unit to be tested, under the command of Major General Raymond 'Tubby' Barton. Alongside the division were the 1st Engineer Special Brigade that had problems during DUCK I. Now switched from OMAHA to UTAH Beach, they were greatly reinforced but were still making up a lot of their equipment since leaving Italy.

REAR ADMIRAL DON MOON – US COMMANDER OF FORCE U. AS SUCH, HE WAS ALSO HEAVILY
INVOLVED IN THE INQUIRY OVER THE LOSS OF LIFE DURING *EXERCISE TIGER*. IT IS SAID HE
NEVER REALLY RECOVERED FROM THE LOSSES SUFFERED AND WENT ON TO TAKE HIS OWN LIFE
DURING AUGUST 1944 IN ITALY PRIOR TO THE LANDINGS IN THE SOUTH OF FRANCE.
(US NAVAL HISTORY & HERITAGE COMMAND)

On the 7th April 1944, Headquarters VII Corps issued the exercise orders. These went to the
4th Infantry Division as the main maritime assault force, but also to both the 82nd and 101st
Airborne Divisions that would jump on D-Day in support of the sea-borne landing, but who
would be trucked-in for the exercise. As with V Corps, VII Corps was to concentrate, marshal
and embark troops in the Plymouth-Tor Bay area, move by sea to Slapton Sands and assault
the beach with both naval gunfire and air support using service scales of live ammunition.

What made TIGER different from FOX was that a large number of very senior visitors had
planned to observe the exercise. These included Generals Eisenhower, Montgomery and
Bradley, the overall naval commander Admiral Ramsey and the Air Force Commander,
Air Marshal Tedder. With them were a large number of others from General Eisenhower's
headquarters. All were keen to see the initial exercise serials, the RAF Typhoon
fighter-bombers strafing and using their 60lb rockets as well as the initial run in to the
beach by the amphibious DD Sherman tanks.

But all was not well. LCTs of the US Navy fell behind time and the opening sequences were delayed by an hour. Unfortunately, this was not relayed to all the assault forces and the second wave landed on time, before the first wave. With troops on the beaches, the planned bombardments had to be cancelled, but here reality becomes conjecture. There are a number of eye witness accounts that quite clearly recall navy shells landing on the beach while it was still occupied by troops. Rumours at the time say upwards of 450 soldiers were killed, but this is most doubtful. If rounds did land on the occupied beach, the firing would have been stopped very quickly.

All day things went wrong, were delayed or simply did not happen. Many of the senior observers were far from impressed when three LCTs equipped with over a 1,000 rockets each came in and fired inland at a series of barbed-wire and pill box targets. Once the smoke cleared it was obvious that many had fallen short, with the smoke and dust blowing out to sea in the off-shore wind, totally obscuring the vision of the launching DD tanks. Unfortunately again, in full view of the seniors, one of the DD tanks promptly sank. If the day was going badly, the night turned decidedly nasty.

Across the English Channel at Cherbourg, the German Navy's 5th and 9th Schnellboote (S-Boats) Flotillas were preparing to put to sea. German intelligence had noted that there had been increased activity in Lyme Bay and along the coast all the way down to Lands End in Cornwall. Orders had been issued for increased patrolling South-West along the English South Coast to see what was happening and interdict any convoys that might be associated with such movements. The 5th Flotilla had already had success in mid-February 1944 around Guernsey, intercepting two convoys and sinking four transport vessels. Then on the 13th April, two boats from the Flotilla sank the Norwegian destroyer Eskdale in a further night action. Thus, on the evening of the 27th April, both Flotillas were feeling brave and bold as they sallied-forth with a combined force of nine S-Boats.

Back on Slapton Sands, the senior observers had left for their hotels and to write up their notes. The exercise called for a follow-up force to move at night and to be landed on the beaches at first light, the 28th April. This was to largely consist of elements of the 1st ESB that had been swapped with the 6th earlier. Two LST convoys set sail from Plymouth and Dartmouth. The first consisted of five vessels – LSTs 515, 496, 511, 531 and 58 – the latter towing two pontoon causeways. The second convoy consisted of three LSTs – 499, 289 and 507. The combined group, known as 'T-4', sailed East up to Brixham and then turned about to sail West back along the coast.

Sometime after 1.30am on the 28th April, the nine German S-Boats from Cherbourg ran into convoy 'T-4'. At least one of the LSTs had its radar on and reportedly picked up two of the German boats approaching but put the 'blips' down to part of the exercise. The German torpedo boats wasted no time. The first LST to be attacked was LST 507 at the rear of the convoy. She was hit by several torpedoes, one of which detonated setting the LST on fire. This rapidly took hold. Five minutes later, she was hit by a second torpedo and had her decks raked with machine-gun fire. Those who had managed to jump ship were also deliberately shot at in the water.

After this pass, a further S-Boat attacked LST-531, hitting her with a torpedo amidships. Those on deck saw flares in the sky and immediately thought they had been attacked from the air. Working their way up along the convoy, the German boats hit the next in line,

LST-511. She was struck by two torpedoes, both of which failed to detonate – a very lucky escape. Finally LST-289 was also hit. The torpedo detonated under her stern, destroying the ship's crew quarters and rudder alongside twisting the rear gun decks from the horizontal into the vertical. The remainder of the convoy had little comprehension of what was happening. The LSTs scattered, increasing their speed although the convoy flag ship, LST-515, did an about turn after some time to pick up survivors. LSTs-507 and 531 burned for two hours, with 531 sinking. A Royal Navy destroyer arrived at about 04.00am to give assistance and decided to sink LST-507, who only had her bow above water.

LST-289 WITH HER STERN BLOWN OFF. (US NATIONAL ARCHIVES & RECORDS ADMINISTRATION)

The casualties from this German attack were high but to this day still questioned. The War Diaries of individual vessels claimed 639 killed and 88 wounded as follows:

LST - 531 424 killed & 25 wounded
LST - 507 202 killed & 24 wounded
LST - 289 13 killed & 21 wounded
LST - 511 18 wounded

In 1946 the official casualty figures were given as 749 killed and 300 wounded, with many of the latter suffering exposure from having been in the sea for a considerable time before rescue. More recent research figures give the number of dead and missing as 1,405. The fall-out of the differing figures points to the fact that the LSTs did not really know who was on board.

Many of the Army who died served within 1st ESB, commanded by Colonel Eugene M. Caffey. As already noted, this brigade had been swapped with the 6th ESB. Of their sub-units, the 3206th Quartermaster Service Company was virtually wiped out, with the official report claiming 201 killed from a full complement of 250 officers and men. Another badly hit unit was the 557th Quartermaster Railhead Company who reportedly suffered 69 casualties in all. Unfortunately, some of the casualties were due to Americans firing at Americans. LST-511 was badly hit by 20mm fire from LST-496 that had steamed off to a flank. The majority of the wounded suffered badly having been hit by these large-calibre rounds.

COLONEL EUGENE M. CAFFEY, COMMANDER OF THE 1ST ENGINEER SPECIAL BRIGADE. DISMISSED FROM COMMAND ON THE SUGGESTION OF GENERAL BRADLEY FOLLOWING THE LOSSES DURING *EXERCISE TIGER.* (UNITED STATES ARMY IN WORLD WAR 2: THE TECHNICAL SERVICES)

Unsurprisingly, the performance of Colonel Caffey and the 1st ESB the following day was none too good. This was immediately noted by both General Collins the VII Corps Commander and General Bradley, the Army Commander. Neither general had a detailed knowledge of the S-Boat attack during the previous night and thus decided that Colonel Caffey should be replaced. It was not until 1951, when General Bradley published his autobiography, that Caffey learnt of the reason why he had been dismissed. He subsequently wrote to the military authorities in Washington and asked for his personal record to be corrected.

*

The final rehearsals for the landings was a series of six planned exercises called FABIUS I to FABIUS VI. These were to cover four of the five assaults and the two follow-up forces, although the UTAH Beach landing was not exercised due to TIGER. Exercises FABIUS I to IV were held simultaneously between the 23rd April and the 7th May under command of Headquarters, 21st Army Group. FABIUS V and VI were held between the 4th and 6th May, coinciding with the landings of the previous four. FABIUS I involved the American 1st and 29th Infantry Division elements that were to land on OMAHA Beach. The force marshalled in Area D and then embarked in harbours between Portland and Weymouth. The landings took place at Slapton Sands.

What set FABIUS aside from all the other exercises was that it was designed to test the complete invasion infrastructure, not the assault forces. The exercises were to resemble Operation NEPTUNE as closely as possible in order to ensure that the higher echelons were tested. The biggest difference from what went before was that the assault troops did not return to their old barracks or concentration areas, instead returning to the marshalling camps. Lessons were learnt but time was running out.

On the 8th May 1944, the Supreme Allied Commander Europe, General Eisenhower, set D-Day for Y-Day plus 4 or the 5th June. Y-Day had initially been set for the 1st May but had been put back to the 1st June some months previously. On the 23rd May, Supreme Headquarters issued a signal to all junior commands to that effect. L-Day was thus set for the 31st May, with all vessels sealed by the 3rd June. At the same time, Eisenhower moved his headquarters to co-locate it with that of Admiral Ramsey – Commander NEPTUNE – at Southwick House, Portsmouth. This was also conveniently close to the combined assault headquarters, also in Portsmouth. General Montgomery had already joined the Headquarters 21st Army Group at HMS Dryad on the 28th April, although his personal quarters were several miles away at Broomfield Park. All was thus set.

*

Between March and June 1944, the West Country quite literally filled up with American troops. The decision to add an extra American assault onto the Far Shore and capture Cherbourg saw a massive growth of the Western Task Force (WTF). A large number of additional landing craft had to be withdrawn from the Mediterranean and additional troops found for VII Corps. Additional SOS units also had to be found in order to reinforce SnBS and its XVIII and XIX Districts. Cornwall bore the brunt of the additional forces since it had the space to accommodate them. Tented camp after tented camp sprang up around Truro and yet more houses and their grounds were requisitioned as continuous streams of men and supplies were squeezed into the county.

Alongside the big exercises FOX, TIGER and FABIUS, other smaller exercises were also ordered on more local beaches. This was particularly important for the US Naval Combat Demolition Units (NCDU) based first in Falmouth and then Fowey.

On the 25th February 1944 USN beach intelligence had reported for the first time that air reconnaissance photographs taken a few days before showed beach obstacles being constructed. These were being built at the mid-point between the spring and neap tide lines and were obviously designed to counter landing craft. Some of these were very basic, merely pit props with an anti tank mine or artillery shell attached to the end, others were more devilish and designed to rip open the hulls of vessels below the waterline. Steel tetrahedrons – or 'hedgehogs' – and obstacles called 'Belgian Gates' were particularly worrisome and would require explosives through which to force gaps for the landing craft.

THE INITIAL GERMAN BEACH OBSTACLES WERE LARGELY STAKES TOPPED WITH ANTI-TANK MINES. OVER A SHORT PERIOD OF TIME, THESE BECAME RAPIDLY MORE SOPHISTICATED UNDER GENERAL ROMMEL. (UNITED STATES ARMY IN WORLD WAR 2: THE TECHNICAL SERVICES)

On the 12th February, 1st Army had already given orders for the formation of the 'Provisional Engineer Special Brigade Group'. This saw the grouping of the 5th and 6th Engineer Special Brigades under one headquarters in order to provide a consolidated team to force gaps off the beaches once ashore at OMAHA. With the profusion of obstacles now appearing on the beaches – nicknamed 'Rommel's Asparagus' – additional teams were needed for their clearance. On the 17th March 1944, V Corps was directed to submit a detailed plan for the removal of the new beach obstacles by 1st April but it was not until the 30th April that V Corps announced the formation of the counter obstacle group.

This consisted of two Army engineer combat battalions, reinforced with Sherman tank bulldozers. In all there would be twenty-one Navy Combat Demolition Units (NCDU) teams to tackle any obstacles that were below the inshore line.

BELGIAN GATES, THE MOST SUBSTANTIAL OF ROMMEL'S BEACH DEFENCES, REQUIRED A TEAM OF FOUR TO DEAL WITH THEM. (CRITICAL PAST)

Between the 31st October 1943 and the 14th February 1944, ten of the new NCDU units arrived in the United Kingdom and were sent South to Falmouth. Here they were equally divided into Groups I, II and III and attached to the 7th, 6th and 2nd Beach Battalions. As such, Group I went on to train at Salcombe, Group II also to Salcombe but then on to Swansea and Group III to Fowey. Between late-February and mid-April, it was the Fowey NCDU teams that were involved in considerable experimental work. Air reconnaissance had noted new obstacles but the new aerial photos were not released for security reasons; they would only become available from 1st May onwards.

While at Fowey, one of the NCDU commanders, Lt Hagensen, developed what became known as the 'Hagensen Pack Charge'. This was a 2lb block of the new C2 plastic explosive in a sown canvas bag with a basic lit fuse. These charges were designed for use against steel obstacles and were found to be very effective. Right up to the point where the NCDU teams went to their marshalling camps, sail-makers in Fowey were to be found hard at work sowing the bags for the explosives charges.

A US NAVAL COMBAT DEMOLITION TEAM TACKLES A 'HEDGEHOG' OBSTACLE – INK AND WASH DRAWING BY MITCHELL F. JAMIESON, 1944. THESE OBSTACLES COMPRISED OF THREE STEEL RAILS RIVETED IN THE MIDDLE WITH THE FEET SPLAYED TO PREVENT SINKING INTO THE SAND. (US NAVAL HISTORY & HERITAGE COMMAND)

*

As the run-up to D-Day fast approached, the South Coast slowly braced itself. In Cornwall, the embarkation points were ready and the marshalling camps prepared. In Falmouth, St Mawes, Fowey and Plymouth, the final American Flotillas arrived from the Mediterranean and moored up.

In St Mawes, SLCU-2 moved into their new hutted camp completed by the 81st Construction Battalion on the 25th April 1944. For a brief period only therefore, it was used on several Saturday nights for dances or ENSA and MSO musical shows. Towards the end of April, the base numbers began to decrease as sections were moved out to join the invasion fleet. This included thirty LCMs and crews that left for their assembly point at Southampton. With everyone moving out, steps were taken to begin the decommissioning of the base. St Mawes was to be one of the first to go and there was no precedent for handing it over to the British Admiralty. As such, issues arose. One of these was the ownership of the base furniture; did it stay with the USN or was it to become the property of the Royal Navy. In the end the decision was made to load as much as possible onto the LCMs and take it all to Southampton for others to consider. On the 15th May 1944, three LCTs arrived and took onboard all the maintenance equipment from Bird's Yard, transporting it to Southampton. Two days later – on the 17th May – the USN relinquished all rights to British land and buildings, allowing the base to be dismantled by the 28th July 1944.

EXERCISE SPLINT WAS DESIGNED TO TEST CASUALTY EVACUATION FROM A BEACH ONTO AN LST PRIOR TO EVACUATION. (US NATIONAL ARCHIVES & RECORDS ADMINISTRATION)

At Fowey in the run-up to D-Day, life was very busy. It had become an out-station of the US base at Plymouth. Not only did it support SLCU-7, it had become a major logistics hub and had been designated as a reception and initial rehabilitation centre for ship crews sunk at sea. Indeed, some of the first rescued crewmen were those rescued during Exercise TIGER. Its importance was emphasised by the visits from Admirals Stark, Kirk and Moon. All training had ceased and the vacated camps were turned over to these men. Given good and plentiful food, fresh milk and access to varied recreational facilities, many began to quickly make the recovery to duty fitness. At the same time, the medical school at Fowey was also heavily involved in preparing for a major medical exercise, practising casualty treatment and evacuation from the beaches out to waiting ships. This was Exercise SPLINT and principally used the beach by Pentewan, in St Austell Bay.

By August 1944, Fowey was more a rehabilitation centre than anything else. As such, it was decided that the spare lodgings available would be ideal for a new base unit – DREW-6 – that was to be established in France. On the 7th August, the unit was formed, many being flown in direct from the United States. Incorporating elements from Fowey, the complete number to move to France consisted of 130 officers along with over a 1,000 NCOs and enlisted men. The 25th August saw the advance party moved to France, followed a month later by the remainder onboard a USN Liberty transport ship. Almost immediately after DREW-6 had gone, a large detachment of the 29th CBs arrived to dismantle the navy huts and make repairs to the civilian housing and hotels that had been requisitioned. By the end of the year Fowey was handed back to the Royal Navy, following the closure of the American base.

In Falmouth, greater and greater numbers of landing-craft of all types, big and small, moored up for their final preparations prior to embarkation. Falmouth, Helford, Fowey and Plymouth West were to load up follow-on Force B, destined to land additional troops onto both the beaches at OMAHA and UTAH between the first and third tides. At the same time, many of the LSTs would be assigned to tow various elements of the proposed artificial breakwaters and the newly designed Rhino Ferries and Tugs. These latter craft had initially been designed at the US Navy's Advanced Base Proving Ground, Davisville on Rhode Island.

ALTHOUGH TAKEN DURING EXERCISE DUCK I, THIS PHOTOGRAPH BEGINS TO SHOW THE BUILD-UP OF VESSELS IN FALMOUTH HARBOUR. LCT-209 IS MOORED UP ALONGSIDE ANOTHER LCT WITH ANOTHER EIGHT MOORED TO STERN. THE LARGE BUILDING ON THE SKY LINE IS LIKELY TO BE THE FALMOUTH HOTEL AND TO THE RIGHT IS THE OLD FALMOUTH GASWORKS. (US NATIONAL ARCHIVES & RECORDS ADMINISTRATION)

Every beach has two elements; the 'approach' and the 'beach' itself. The 'approach' constitutes the part of the beach uncovered at 'low-water-springs' but covered at 'high-water-neaps' with the 'beach' being that which lies between 'high-water-springs' and 'high-water-neaps'. In order to land on the average beach, the standard LST was designed with a keel gradient of one in fifty, three feet deep at the bow and nine feet deep at the stern. Thus, on landing at a beach with a similar gradient, LSTs could off-load immediately. The selected Normandy beaches had an average 'approach' of nearly a quarter of a mile with a gradient of one in three hundred, with the 'beach' having a gradient of one in forty. As such, assault landings could only really be undertaken during the high-water of Spring tides. Any other tides would mean that LSTs would run their sterns aground with eight feet of water at the bow. Consequently, some form of floating platform was required to cover the last 400 yards or so.

AMERICAN PONTOON LIGHTERAGE BOXES TYPE–6 (L) AND A TAPERED TYPE–7. AKIN TO MODERN–DAY 'LEGO', THESE BOXES WERE USED TO BUILD ANY NUMBER OF DIFFERING FLOATING PLATFORMS OF WHICH THE 'RHINO FERRY' WAS TO BECOME SYNONYMOUS WITH AMPHIBIOUS LANDINGS. (US NAVAL HISTORY & HERITAGE COMMAND)

The concept behind the Rhino Ferry (RHF) was a 'pontoon', a water-tight floating steel cuboid box measuring 7ft x 5ft x 5ft and called a T6 Naval Lighterage (NL) unit. These were designed to be bolted together in long strings or one on top of the other, forming floating platforms. Separate T7 units with one side curved could be bolted onto the for'ard end of any platform to form a bow. Such a platform was first used in 1937 by a Californian mining company to move a dredger. In 1940-1941, the US Navy built its first experimental model out of cigar boxes and wooden struts. Each T6 could float in 18 inches of water and ultimately support five and a half tons while a completed ferry would hold 300 tons and had a draught of three feet.

A RHINO TUG UNDER CONSTRUCTION IN FALMOUTH. THESE TUGS USED SPECIALLY DESIGNED ENGINE UNITS WHILE THEIR LARGER COUSINS, THE RHINO FERRIES, USED OUTBOARD ENGINES. (US NATIONAL ARCHIVES & RECORDS ADMINISTRATION)

CONSTRUCTING A RHINO FERRY IN FALMOUTH OR PLYMOUTH. NOTE THE UPTURNED PROPELLER DRIVE SHAFTS. LIEUTENANT COMMANDER DWIGHT SHEPLER, LATE SPRING 1944. (US NAVAL HISTORY & HERTIAGE COMMAND-SHEPLER)

ABLE TO MOVE 300 TONS OF LIGHTERAGE AT A TIME, A RHINO FERRY OFF-LOADS ELEMENTS OF AN AMERICAN SHERMAN TANK COMPANY ONTO OMAHA BEACH, JUNE 1944. (US NAVY CB MUSEUM ARCHIVE)

To power the ferries, twin General Motors O2D or Gray-Marine diesel engines were used, providing some 350 horse-power. About the size of a tractor engine, these outboards were, for their time, the largest and most powerful in the world. They were also able to be rotated out of the water, propellers uppermost, for servicing. Each Rhino Ferry used 180 'pontoons' and was 176ft long and 42ft wide. It covered some 6,000 sq.ft. with a 20ft ramp for'ard for the discharge of cargo. On the stern of the ferry, there were two timber braces designed to lock with the standard LST ramp, allowing the latter to unload directly onto a ferry at sea.

The first shipment of pontoons arrived in the country on the 15th November and a detachment of the 81st CB in Falmouth was set to work to build the first ferry, a Rhino Tug. This was finished just after the 1st December whereupon production of the first Rhino Ferry immediately commenced. The Falmouth construction yard was 'side-launching' with the capacity of only one pontoon string thirty units long. The yard was dry at low tide and all new pontoons arriving from America had to be unloaded through the yard. As such, two further yards were searched for along the South Coast. One was found in Plymouth and another in Dartmouth, with both in operation by January 1944.

At the beginning of 1944, the 1006th CB Detachment (CBD) and the 111th CB arrived to support the 81st CB, the former from the Mediterranean and the latter from the United States. The 1006th CBD had been used to lay floating pontoon causeways across the beaches in both Sicily and Italy. 111th CB sent detachments to all three pontoon construction yards as well as sending a small group to Southampton to support British Royal Engineers who were also building ferries. By June 1944, additional battalions and detachments were employed in a wide variety of pontoon construction.

For D-Day, twenty-seven tugs and ferries were planned for and were completed by the 25th April. At the same time the Americans began an experimental programme looking at floating causeways, starting at the beginning of February 1944. This was undertaken in Par Harbour with the causeways designed to allow shallow-draft vessels to unload dry-shod. These causeways consisted of a series of 2 x 30 pontoon strings attached end to end and then sunk on to a flat beach. Along these causeways were also attached much larger landing platforms made up of four strings of twelve pontoons and called 'blisters'. These were set 350 feet apart along each side of the causeway. While building both the Rhinos and the causeways, CB personnel were also being trained to man these platforms as they were to take them across the Channel with the invasion fleet, towed behind either a LCT or LST.

LIEUTENANT COMMANDER SHEPLER PAINTED 'SEABEES' ATTACHING AN OFF–LOADING RAMP
CALLED A 'PLATYPUS' TO AN LST IN FALMOUTH. IN THE BACKGROUND IS TAYLOR'S GARAGE.
(US NAVAL HISTORY & HERITAGE COMMAND - SHEPLER)

7

'LET'S GO…'

I n the middle of May 1944, the 29th Infantry Division, its attached support units and the accompanying Engineer Special Brigade Group units all upped-sticks and moved into their Marshalling Areas. Many believed this was yet another exercise, but others noted the tighter security and sheer weight of troops and equipment all about. The units within their camps were split up into their boat-loads. With this came the detailed briefings, although in most cases the real names of towns along with their grid references were not used, as final orders could only be opened onboard the landing craft.

One major problem solved only at the last moment was the lack of personnel to service the assaulting troops in the 'sausage camps', particularly cooks and logistics staff. After much strife, it was decided to order the 5th US Armoured Division into Cornwall from Wiltshire to assist in running the camps. Having only arrived in the UK during February 1944, the 5th Armoured moved into the camps around Truro, Plymouth and Torquay in early April 1944.

In order to undertake this new tasking, the Division reorganised itself. The Division's two tank battalions (minus their vehicles) along with the engineer battalion, went into the Truro area while the artillery headquarters and artillery battalions occupied the camps to the West of Plymouth. In particular, each company group had to run up to six 'messes' and corresponding kitchens. Volunteers were called for from the tank crews and infantry to undertake a crash cooking course. The response was overwhelming with the infantry battalions passing out 72 cooks at Grade 1. When not looking after those in the camps as they moved onto the embarkation hards, the 5th Armoured Division personnel were allowed local leave into towns such as Redruth, Truro and Chacewater with the local population opening up their evening clubrooms for those off-duty soldiers.

*

On the night of the 29th and 30th May, German bombers attacked Falmouth in what was to be the last raid of the war in the county. The Germans had mustered a relatively large force of fifty-one aircraft, of which thirty were to attack Falmouth. A further two went to St Austell as a diversion, while the remaining nineteen aircraft were to drop mines in the approaches to the River Fal. The Air Raid sirens sounded at 00.21am when the raid was detected some 30-35 miles South of Falmouth. Eight minutes later, green flares were dropped across the port and town and the anti-aircraft guns began firing. In all, some 30 metric tons of bombs were dropped.

Several bombs hit important targets. The Pentargon and Boscowen Hotels received direct hits, killing 5 and wounding 18. Ironically the Headquarters of the RAF's 959 Barrage Balloon Squadron in Falmouth was badly damaged next door. Outside of the town, the Swanpool oil and fuel installation was also hit. One of the fuel tanks ruptured and immediately caught fire, spilling burning oil into a local stream close to a row of houses. The fire burned for twenty-two hours, despite all the efforts by both the Falmouth Fire Brigade and US naval volunteers, some of whom were from the USNAAB Fire Fighting Team. Two American bulldozers were brought in to dam-up the stream, for which the two American operators were awarded the British Empire Medal. One of the recipients, Bosun's Mate Philip Bishop, went on to marry a local Cornish lady and settled in Seattle at the end of the war.

THE BOSCOWEN (L) AND PENTARGON (R) HOTELS, FALMOUTH, BOMBED IN THE EARLY HOURS OF THE 30TH MAY 1944, KILLING FIVE AND WOUNDING 18. (CORNISH STUDIES LIBRARY)

In the surrounding countryside, now packed with marshalled troops waiting to board their landing craft from their 'sausage camps', a large bomb hit the temporary garage of the 3516th Ordnance Medium Automobile Maintenance Company, that had been undertaking immediate vehicle repairs for those troops waiting to load. The single bomb killed five and wounded another three while they slept.

*

Despite the worsening weather, L-Day remained the 31st May 1944. Having been cooped-up in their marshalling camps for some time, at last the assault troops were brought forward to their embarkation hards. Follow-on Force B, known as Task Force 126 (TF-126), was made up of troops due to land on both OMAHA and UTAH immediately behind the assault force.

Commanded by Commodore C.D. Edgar and based out of Plymouth, TF-126 consisted of four convoys; three 'slow' convoys travelling at five knots and one fast, travelling at twelve knots. Convoys B-1 out of Plymouth and Fowey, B-3 from Falmouth and Helford and U-4 from Salcombe in Devon were 'slow' due to having to tow Rhino Ferries or Tugs, Causeway sections, Gooseberry or Mulberry Harbour elements across the Channel. Convoy B-2 was a fast convoy, leaving from Plymouth on D-Day itself. All four convoys were due to sortie-out at D minus 1(D-1) with B-1 heading for Utah and B-2 for Omaha. Both were due to be off-shore by the second tide on D-Day. B-3 and U-4 were to merge off Salcombe and became Convoy ECL-1. Although each individual vessel within the convoy had a designated beach which to approach, this was to be confirmed at the time.

Loading Force B was a complicated business due to the number of harbours being used. LST loading was split into four Loading Groups, from A to D. Each ship was ordered to sail to a holding harbour prior to being called forward to its hard. Once loaded, the vessel was ordered to a mooring position in the harbour from which it would sail. At each hard LST loading was further broken down in to groups, with each vessel given only six hours to embark its assigned loads. Each Cornish hard loaded the following LSTs:

Polgerran Wood, River Fal (PF-1):
- Group A – LSTs 54, 212, 497, 5 and 386.
- Group B – LSTs 61, 307, 292, 393 and 306.

Turnaware Point, River Fal (PF-2):
- Group A – LSTs 331*, 392, 355, 7 and 356.
- Group B – LST 389.
- Group C – LSTs 391 and 53.
- Group D – LSTs 523, 59, 338, 325 and 336.

Helford River, Falmouth (PH):
- Group A – LSTs 532, 27*, 266, 369, 335 and 516.
- Group B – LSTs 28, 533, 262*, 538, 16* and 337.

Upper Barnpool, Plymouth (PP-1):
- Group A – LSTs 495, 494, 55, 498, 291, 496 and 512.
- Group B – LSTs 288, 504, 56, 510, 506, 511 and 505.

(All LSTs denoted thus * were crewed by the US Coast Guard)

TOP: THE SWANPOOL OIL AND FUEL INSTALLATION BURNING AFTER THE GERMAN RAID IN THE EARLY HOURS OF 30TH MAY 1944. IT TOOK A LARGE NUMBER OF MEN AND MANY HOURS TO BRING UNDER CONTROL. (US NATIONAL ARCHIVES & RECORDS ADMINITSRATION)

BOTTOM: THERE ARE FEW PHOTOS OF GALLANTRY MEDALS BEING WON. BOSUN'S MATE PHILLIP BISHOP PHOTOGRAPHED AS HE DAMS THE RUNNING RIVLETS OF BURNING FUEL-OIL POURING FROM A RUPTURED TANK AT SWANPOOL. (US NATIONAL ARCHIVES & RECORDS ADMINISTRATION)

TOP: LSTs–533 AND 27 UPLOADING FOR D-DAY. INTERESTINGLY, LST–27 WAS CREWED BY THE US COAST GUARD, ONE OF ONLY FOUR SUCH VESSELS WITHIN TASK FORCE 126. (CRITICAL PAST)

BOTTOM: A SERIES OF US HALF–TRACKS LOADING ONTO LST–28 AT POLGWYDDEN (TREBAH) HARD ON THE 1ST JUNE 1944. SOME 80 VEHICLES AND 471 PERSONNEL WERE LOADED PRIOR TO MOORING AT KING HARRY FERRY. LST–28 SAILED FOR NORMANDY WITH CONVOY B-3. (CRITICAL PAST)

The convoys for Force B sailed from a number of different ports and harbours having loaded. Their numbers were also increased with the addition of both LCTs, LCI(L)s and the tows out of Falmouth. With H-Hour being 06.30am on D-Day, the three Cornish convoys making up Force B sailed as follows:

Convoy B-1 – sailed from Plymouth and Fowey with a total of 14 x LSTs and 46 x LCTs from the former and 4 x LSTs from the latter. The convoy speed was set at 5 knots and the ships were to pass the Eddystone Lighthouse by H-26 hours. The convoy formed up with two columns of LSTs flanked either side by a column of LCTs.

Convoy B-2 – sailed from Plymouth with a total of 32 x LSTs, 46 x LCTs and 6 x LCI(L)s, the latter to sail at the head of the convoy as it was destined to land as quickly as possible on OMAHA Beach. The convoy speed was to be 13 knots and they were to be abreast of the Eddystone Lighthouse by H-5 hours.

Convoy B-3 – sailed from Falmouth, Helford and Fowey, with a total of 34 x LSTs with the Falmouth vessels towing a total 42 x tows. An additional 9 x LSTs sailed for UTAH Beach from Salcombe as convoy 'U-4'. The convoy speed was 5 knots with U-4 as the 'tail-end charlies' passing the Eddystone Lighthouse at H-10 hours.

Each craft was ordered to carry sufficient fuel to ensure that on landing in Normandy, the LST had the correct trim. Each LST also only transported six LCV(P)/LCMs per ship. On reaching the initial anchorage off-shore, these were lowered and went off to rendezvous with their pre-designated LSTs and LCI(L)s. Force B carried both the 26th RCT from the 1st Infantry Division and the 175th RCT from the 29th. These required 78 and 77 LCV(P)s apiece in order to take the troops ashore.

TROOPS OF 30TH CHEMICAL DECONTAMINATION COMPANY, 6TH SPECIAL ENGINEER BRIGADE 'LOCKED DOWN' ON BOARD LST-325. THE LARGE BOARD WITH '474 O' IS AN ARMY LOADING SERIAL NUMBER, WITH THE 'O' DENOTING OMAHA BEACH. ST MAWES CASTLE CAN BE SEEN IN THE RIGHT BACKGROUND OF THE PHOTOGRAPH AND THE FLY WHEEL AND CABLE ATTACHMENT AT THE BOTTOM OF THE PICTURE IS THE BALLOON TETHERING MECHANISM.
(US NAVAL HISTORY & HERITAGE COMMAND)

MULBERRY A – THE AMERICAN ARTIFICIAL HARBOUR, SO BADLY DAMAGED BY THE JUNE 1944 STORM THAT IT WAS ABANDONED AND ALL OPERATIONS SWITCHED TO MULBERRY B OFF THE BRITISH BEACHES. (US NAVAL HISTORY & HERITAGE COMMAND)

As is now well known, the first attempt to launch the invasion was delayed by General Eisenhower for 24 hours due to the bad weather. In June 1944, the Atlantic witnessed weather more akin to winter than summer, with a series of depressions moving West to East across Southern England and Northern France. All were hoping for a benign period with the wind between 10 to 15 knots and no heavy swell. Both the navies and the air forces hoped for broken cloud above 1,000 ft and visibility from 3 to 5 miles. This was not to be. On the 3rd June, Group Captain JM Stagg RAF briefed General Eisenhower that the weather was worsening. He was right and at 04.15am on the 4th June, his briefing convinced all that the invasion should be delayed by at least twenty-four hours. That evening, Stagg again briefed Eisenhower, noting that there might be a weather gap. This was enough and Eisenhower made his decision; D-Day would be the 6th June, 1944.

Had Eisenhower further delayed the landings, the next appropriate tidal period would have been the 19th June. What actually transpired was the largest Channel storm for decades. This destroyed the American Mulberry harbour and wreaked havoc amongst the myriad craft off the Normandy coast. It also delayed the arrival of further troops and equipment for three days, a vital time during the build on the beaches. Had General Eisenhower postponed the landings on the 4th June to the 19th, the storm would have postponed it yet again.

Eisenhower's last minute and bold decision to go was always fraught with danger, as the landings on OMAHA Beach demonstrated. Throughout the 6th June he carried a small piece of paper in his jacket pocket. On it he had written the following:

"Our landings in the Cherbourg-Havre area have failed to gain a satisfactory foothold and I have withdrawn the troops. My decision to attack at this time and place was based upon the best information available. The troops, the air and the Navy did all that Bravery (sic) and direction to duty could do. If any blame is found attached to this attempt it is mine alone."

Eisenhower had been so nervous at the time that he dated it the 5th July.

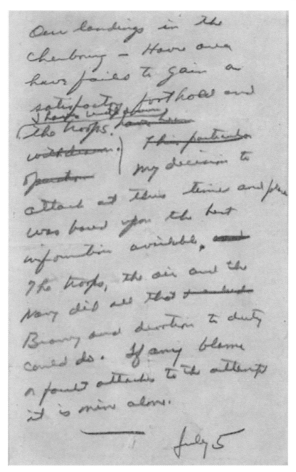

GENERAL EISENHOWER'S PLANNED MESSAGE, SHOULD
THE TROOPS DURING OPERATION NEPTUNE FAIL TO
GAIN A SUBSTANTIAL FOOTHOLD IN NORMANDY.
(EISENHOWER PRESIDENTIAL LIBRARY)

8

'A BROTHERHOOD IN ARMS'

At noon on the 6th June 1944, Prime Minister Churchill rose in the House of Commons. He taunted the packed benches before him by first describing the Allied successes in Italy, especially the fall of Rome. No doubt pausing for effect, Churchill continued:

'I have also to announce to the House that during the night and the early hours of this morning the first of a series of landings in force upon the European continent has taken place. In this case, the liberating assault fell upon the coast of France...'

The Prime Minister went on to give brief details of the initial landings and promised that the assault troops would be constantly reinforced in the weeks ahead. He went on to say:

'Complete unity prevails throughout the Allied Armies. There is a brotherhood in arms between us and our friends of the United States. There is complete confidence in the Supreme Commander, General Eisenhower, and his lieutenants, and also in the commander of the Expeditionary Force, General Montgomery. The ardour and spirit of the troops...embarking in these last few days was splendid to witness'.

For the Americans, it was the effort put in by the Service of Supply, and in particular the XVIII and XIX Districts of the Southern Base Section, that ensured many of the critical facets of the American NEPTUNE plan were the success that they were. On the 6th June alone, SnBS processed 80,000 troops. In the month of June, SnBS moved 51,800 tons of supplies and 60,000 vehicles across the Channel. The SnBS history proudly mentions that they moved the entire 83rd Infantry Division and its equipment to France in three days. They also built 38 hospitals between January and June 1944, providing 45,000 beds for the wounded. By the end of June, 27,000 wounded had been through the system, with some 7,000 having been flown in and 1,000 being Prisoners of War.

As the Allies pushed on in France, the SnBS duties fell away. This was especially so once bases were established in France. At this point, SnBS and its Districts turned their hand to Plan RHUMBA, a reverse-BOLERO in which many installations and personnel were released back to their previous owners and employers. Where manpower was still required, the Americans greatly increased the number of Women's Army Corps (WAC), known throughout as the 'G.I Janes'. In addition to these ladies, there was also a huge increase in the employment of volunteer Italian prisoners. These prisoners were divided up into depot labour gangs, issued British uniforms with the shoulder flash 'Italy' sown onto the shoulders.

On the 19th June 1944, orders went out that XIX District was to begin closing down. This was further emphasised on the 1st September when it was announced that the Service of Supply troops in the United Kingdom would become the United Kingdom Base Section. SnBS was dissolved and renamed Southern District.

For Cornwall, the launch of the invasion really saw the end of the county's involvement. By the 1st October, USNAAB Falmouth turned itself wholly over to the repair of landing ships and other naval craft damaged in action or by storm. The Base history also suggests that there was a fall-off in morale following the invasion; the excitement had gone to be replaced by monotony.

FALMOUTH SHIP REPAIR AT ITS MOST EXTREME. THE SURVIVING FORWARD SECTIONS OF LST-599 IN DRY-DOCK FOR REPAIR AFTER BEING TORPEDOED IN AUGUST 1944 OFF THE NORTH CORNWALL COAST. (ROYAL CORNWALL POLYTECHNIC SOCIETY)

POSTSCRIPT

The success of Operations NEPTUNE and OVERLORD, planned, practised and executed from Southern England was due to the Anglo-American partnership and co-operation that built and honed the forces that dealt the final blow. Today, British history tends to ignore the fact that the Americans were responsible for the major share of the fighting in Western Europe. More importantly, the Americans largely bank-rolled the whole endeavour. For Roosevelt, the bed-rock of the Anglo-American co-operation had been Lend-Lease and Reverse Lend-Lease. In all, the United States paid out some $50.1 billion or 17% of its total war effort to a myriad of nations (roughly equating to some $667 billion today). Of this $31.4 billion went to the British. In return, the United States accepted some $7.8 billion-worth of goods and services of which $6.8 billion came from the United Kingdom and Dominion countries. At the time the United Kingdom might have been selling itself cheaply; Reverse Lend-Lease gave the Americans radar, sonar, RF fuses, engine superchargers, plastic explosives, gyroscopic gunsights and dedicated support for the Manhattan Project that ended the war in the Pacific in August 1945.

Nigh-on seventy-five years have passed since large numbers of American soldiers, sailors and airman crowded the villages and towns of Cornwall. Six years after the end of World War 2, British, Dominion and American Forces were again fighting together in Korea. British troops went on to counter communist insurgencies in Malaya, Borneo and oversee independence in a multitude of former colonies. More recently they have operated in Northern Ireland, the Falkland Islands and the Balkans; the list is long and will continue to grow. For the Americans, after Korea they found themselves sucked into Vietnam, Beirut, Cuba, Central America and Grenada.

Most importantly, Britain and America stood together in the forty-five years it took to face down the Warsaw Pact during the Cold War, only to have it replaced by Iraq and Afghanistan, where new generations of mothers and fathers, wives and husbands and girlfriends and boyfriends watched and waited as their loved ones went off to war. Indeed, since 1945 there has only been one year – 1968 – in which a British soldier has not been killed in action.

Throughout the past seventy-five years, the one golden thread running through the military histories of our countries has been the so-called 'special relationship' between London and Washington. Forged by Churchill and Roosevelt, it has endured, kept alive by the continued friendships that can be traced back to the dark days of 1942. One should also remember that 100,000 British women married Americans and emigrated to the US in the ten years between 1942 and 1952.

In Cornwall, year after year, groups of former American servicemen and their families return to remember and pay respects to the memories of their friends who crossed the Channel only to remain there. Tolverne, Trebah, Falmouth, Fowey, Plymouth and of course Slapton Sands, remain very real to them. And when those that served are no longer with us, their children and their childrens' children will undoubtedly continue to return to Cornwall to remember and learn of and from those most remarkable years.

- ARCHIVE SOURCES -

NATIONAL ARCHIVES (TNA), KEW, LONDON:

Admiralty Files:
ADM 1/13220   – US Bases in Plymouth Command
ADM 1/13236   – US Landing Craft & Repair Organisation
ADM 1/13398   – RN HO/TO of Bases to USN
ADM 1/16107   – Closure of USN Bases
ADM 1/29762   – British awards to USN Personnel
ADM 179/338   – US Bases in UK
ADM 179/462   – Operation NEPTUNE – Force B – May 1944
ADM 199/1555 – Miscellaneous D-Day Papers
ADM 199/1576 – D-Day Western Task Force – Various papers 1943-1944
ADM 199/1569 – Operation NEPTUNE – Force B Orders
ADM 199/1570 – Operation NEPTUNE – Home Port Orders
ADM 199/1576 – D-Day WTF Miscellaneous Papers – 1943-1944
ADM 199/1625 – Miscellaneous D-Day Orders – 1944

Cabinet Office Files:
CAB 84/92 – ROUND UP Administrative Planning Staff 1942

Combined Operations Files:
DEFE 2/939C – US Requests for Embarkation Sites – 1942

Home Office Files:
HO 192/923 – Falmouth Bombing – May 1944

Royal Air Force Files:
AIR 27/2310 – War Diary, 959 Balloon Squadron, RAF (1940 to 1945)

War Office Files:
WO 166/762   – HQ Devon & Cornwall Division – G Branch – 1941
WO 166/971   – HQ 73 Independent Infantry Brigade – 1941
WO 166/1056   – HQ 203 Infantry Brigade – Mar-Jul 1941
WO 166/1252   – HQ South-West Area – 1939-1941
WO 166/2229   – HQ South-West District & US D-Day Plans – 1943-1944
WO 166/10904 – HQ South-West District – 1943
WO 166/10949 – HQ Cornwall Sub-District – 1943
WO 166/14220 – HQ Q (Movements) – Southern Command – 1943
WO 166/14450 – HQ South-West District – 1944
WO 166/14483 – HQ Cornwall Sub-District – 1944
WO 166/16522 – HQ South-West District – 1945
WO 166/16548 – HQ Cornwall Sub-District – 1945
WO 199/1161   – HQ Fixed Defences, Falmouth – Jun 1941 to Aug 1944
WO 199/2036   – HQ Southern Command – Order of Battle – 1940-1941
WO 199/2136   – Chief Engineer, HQ Southern Command – 1940-1941
WO 199/2227   – D-Day Camps (K to O) – 1944
WO 199/2229   – Operation NEPTUNE – Joint UK-US Planning – 1944
WO 199/2263   – LST Hards Demolition Planning – 1942-1943
WO 199/2264   – Royal Engineer Road Services – 1942
WO 199/2268   – HQ South-West Loading Hards – Dec 1943
WO 199/2338   – Operation OVERLORD – Route Reconnaissance – Area M

WO 199/2347 – Operation OVERLORD – South-West District Royal Engineers
WO 199/2411 – Operation OVERLORD – Camp Camouflage Checks – 1944

CORNWALL COUNTY ARCHIVES:
AD893/1   – Sea Chart, Fowey Harbour – May 1945
AD906   – Ordnance Survey Plans – Cornwall Bombings – c1945
AD1154   – Territorial Army, 56th (Cornwall) Anti-Aircraft Brigade – 1938-1939
AD2081/1   – Female services personnel, Falmouth – March to September 1944
CC/23/3/2   – (Multiple files) Cornwall Bombings – 1940-1951
CC/POL/68   – (Multiple files) War Diaries, Cornwall County Constabulary – 1939-1945
FYHC/6/5 to 11– Fowey Harbour Log Books – 1939-1945
FYHC/14   – Fowey Harbour Vessels – 1918-1946

CORNISH STUDIES LIBRARY, REDRUTH:
The George Ellis Photographic Archive

FALMOUTH HISTORY ARCHIVE, ROYAL CORNWALL POLYTECHNIC SOCIETY:
V Files – Numerous Falmouth files & photographs – 1939-1945

AMERICAN PRESIDENCY PROJECT – FRANKLIN D. ROOSEVELT 1933-1945:
Eisenhower Presidential Library, Museum & Boyhood Home – Eisenhower's Pre-Presidential Papers,
Principal File, Box 168, Butcher Diary June 28 – July 14, 1944 (2); NAID #186470
First US Army – Report of Operations in the Invasion of Normandy, France, 10/20/43-8/1/44 – Annex
Three, Station List (1944)

US MILITARY HISTORY COMMAND:

Geographical Command Reports:
File 569i   – 3516 Ordnance Medium Automotive Maintenance Company – Unit Historical Record

Historical Section, US European Theatre of Operations (ETOUSA):
File 190   – Leigh Material
File 216   – Planning the Invasion
File 601   – Southern Base Section History, August 1943 – August 1944

Staff Section Reports, US European Theatre of Operations (ETOUSA) - Navy History:
File 341A – Transport Corps, Southern Base Section Historical Note – 6 June 1943
File 562   – US Navy Bases in the United Kingdom 1944
File 547   – Engineers – Chronology of Events – 1941-1945

US Naval History & Heritage Command (NHHC):
13th Naval Construction Regiment – Historical Information
81st Naval Construction Battalion – Historical Information

US Naval War Diaries:
USNAAB Falmouth – 10/13/43 to 30/01/44

GERMAN ARCHIVES
'Luftwaffe and Allied Air Forces Discussion Forum' (online) Available at
http://forum.12oclockhigh.net/archive/index.php?t-2483.html

- IMAGE SOURCES -

Cornish Studies Library

Critical Past: (www.criticalpast.com)

Eisenhower Presidential Library: (www.eisenhower.archives.gov/research/online_documents)

Falmouth History Archive, via Royal Cornwall Polytechnic Society (RCPS)

Ike Skelton Combined Arms Research Library

Imperial War Museum

Tavistock Museum Archive

The Hyper Text Histories – HyperWar: (www.ibiblio.org/hyperwar)

To Those Who Served: (http://tothosewhoserved.org/usa)

United States Army in World War 2: The Technical Services

US Library of Congress – Prints and Photographs Online Catalog: (www.loc.gov/pictures)

US National Archives & Records Administration – Archives Library Information Centre – Digital Photography Collections: (www.archives.gov/research/alic/reference/photography)

US Naval History & Heritage Command (NHHC) – Photography: (www.history.navy.mil/our-collections/photography.html)

US Navy CB Museum Archive: (https://seabeemuseum.wordpress.com)

LIEUTENANT COMMANDER DWIGHT SHEPLER SKETCHING.
(US NAVAL HISTORY & HERITAGE COMMAND)

BIBLIOGRAPHY

Acton, V & Carter, D. *Operation Cornwall 1940-1944* (Devoran: Landfall Publications – 1994)

Balkoski, J.M. *D-Day Encyclopaedia – 29th Infantry Division* (Oxford: Helicon Publishing Ltd – 1994)

Bass, R. *EXERCISE TIGER The D-Day practice landing exercises uncovered* (Brighton: Menin House
    Publishers Reprint 2012)

Bennett G.H. *Destination Normandy – Three American Regiments on D-Day* (Mechanicsburg: Stackpole Books)

Breakell, B. *Falmouth at War* (Launceston: Amigo Books – 1990)

Brown, N.G. *D-Day Encyclopaedia – Weather* (Oxford: Helicon Publishing Ltd – 1994)

Buckton, H. *Friendly Invasion – Memories of Operation BOLERO* (Chichester: Phillimore & Co. Ltd – 2006)

Churchill, W.S. *Into Battle* (London: Cassell & Co. Ltd – 1941)

Churchill, W.S. *The Unrelenting Struggle* (London: Cassell & Co. Ltd – 1942)

Churchill, W.S. *The Second World War* (London: Cassell & Co. Ltd – Revised 1949)

Cline, R. *United States Army in World War 2 – Washington Command Post: The Operations Division* (Centre of
    Military History United States Army)

Crowley, L. *Lend-Lease* (Chicago: Encyclopaedia Britannica Inc – 1947)

Daily Telegraph *Story of the War, September 1941 to December 1942* (London: Hodder & Stoughton – 1943)

De Bevoise, C.P. *VoDo – History of the 81st Tank Battalion* (www.5ad.org)

Eisenhower, D. *Crusade in Europe* (London: William Heineman – Reprinted 1949)

Ellis, Major L.F. *Victory in the West – Vol 1 – The Battle for Normandy* (London: HMSO – 1962)

Falmouth Packet *Widow of Hero of German Bomb Attack dies at 98* (2015)

Gardner, R.S. *Paths of Armor* (US 5th Armored Division) (Nashville: Battery Press)

Gilbert, M *Road to Victory – Winston S. Churchill – 1941-1945* (London: Heineman – 1986)

Hancock, P. *Cornwall at War 1939-1945* (Wellington: Halsgrove (Reprint) – 2007)

Harrison, G. *The US Army in World War 2 – European Theatre of Operations – Cross-Channel Attack*
    (via www.ibiblio.org/hyperwar – 1950)

His Majesty's Stationary Office:
    - Navy List – February 1943
    - Navy List – June 1943

Houterman, H. & Koppes, J. *World War 2 Unit Histories & Officers* (www.unithistories.com)

Hoyt, E.P. *The Invasion Before Normandy – The Secret Battle of Slapton Sands* (London: Robert Hale Ltd –
    Paperback 1988)

Hunt, Maj E. *Rhino Ferries Manned by Sappers and SeaBees* (The Royal Engineers Journal, Volume 127,
    No.3 – 2013)

Ismay, H. *Memoirs of the Lord Ismay KG, PC, GCB, CH, DSO* (London: William Heineman – 1960)

Jones, C.L. *The Administrative and Logical History of the ETO – Part VI – Neptune Training, Mounting [and] The
    Artificial Ports* (via www.ibiblio.org/hyperwar – 1946)

Lewis, N. *Exercise TIGER: The Dramatic True Story of a Hidden Tragedy of World War 2* (New York: Prentice-
    Hall – 1990)

Mead, Lt Col C.J.H. *Cornwall's Royal Engineers* (Plymouth: Underhill (Plymouth) – 1948)

Rogers, J.D. *US Navy SeaBees During World War 2* (Online Presentation via web.mst.edu)

Symonds, C.L. *Operation NEPTUNE* (New York: Oxford University Press – 2014)

US Naval History & Heritage Command (NHHC) – Navy Department Library:
    - Operation NEPTUNE: The Invasion of Normandy
    - Seabee History: Formation of the SeaBees and World War 2 (Fort Hueneme Museum)
    - United States Naval Administration in World War 2. Volume V – The Invasion of Normandy
    - Building the Navy's Bases in World War 2, Volume II (Part III), The Advance Bases, Chapter
        XXI, France and Germany
    - Report of the Naval Demolition Units – Lt HL Blackwell 1944